ACADEMIC LANGUAGE LITERACY

ACADEMIC LANGUAGE LITERACY

Developing Instructional Leadership Skills for Principals and Teachers

Marjorie C. Ringler

ROWMAN & LITTLEFIELD
Lanham • Boulder • New York • London

Published by Rowman & Littlefield
A wholly owned subsidiary of
The Rowman & Littlefield Publishing Group, Inc.
4501 Forbes Boulevard, Suite 200, Lanham, Maryland 20706
www.rowman.com

Unit A, Whitacre Mews, 26-34 Stannary Street, London SE11 4AB

Copyright 2015 by Marjorie C. Ringler

All rights reserved. No part of this book may be reproduced in any form or by any electronic or mechanical means, including information storage and retrieval systems, without written permission from the publisher, except by a reviewer who may quote passages in a review.

British Library Cataloguing in Publication Information Available

Library of Congress Cataloging-in-Publication Data Available

ISBN 978-1-4758-1108-7 (hardcover)
ISBN 978-1-4758-1109-4 (paperback)
ISBN 978-1-4758-1110-0 (ebook)

I dedicate this book to my colleague and friend, Debra O'Neal, who died in April 2013.

Through our years of delivering professional development and research we formed a strong professional and personal friendship with many friends in eastern North Carolina and the nation. Together we wrote the conceptual framework for this book, which now I wrote, to continue a very important message that we both worked so hard to integrate in our circle of influence:

"All learners—regardless of proficiency in their dialects or Standard English—must be proficient in Academic English to be successful in academic settings" (O'Neal and Ringler 2010).

More than a colleague, Debbie was a friend. I miss her and think of her every day! I am thankful for all that she taught me about linguistics, professionalism, and friendship.

CONTENTS

	Preface	xi
1	Effective Professional Development: A Three-Pronged Approach	1
	Content: Academic Language Matters	2
	Conventions of Standard English	3
	Features of Academic Language	4
	So What Is Academic Language?	5
	Context: Creating Chief Education Officers (CEOs)	7
	Am I a CEO or Do I Need to Work on This?	8
	Process: Job-Embedded Coaching and Collaboration	11
	Phase One: Preparation and Planning	11
	Phase Two: Implementation and Reflection	11
	Phase Three: Capacity Building	13
	Summary	13
	Works Cited	14
2	Content: What Comprises Academic Language Literacy (ALL)?	15
	Components of Academic Language	17
	Process/Function Words	17
	Morphology	18
	Content-Specific Vocabulary	20
	Who Needs Academic Language Literacy?	22

	Group #1: Native Speakers of English or Standard English Learners (SELs)	22
	Group #2: English Language Learners (ELLs)	23
	How Do We Deliver Academic Language Instruction?	25
	An Overview of SIOP®, CHATS, and Six-Steps	26
	Connecting the Dots: How Do These Three Models Overlap?	31
	Summary	31
	Works Cited	33
3	Content: Specific Strategies for Academic Language Literacy	35
	Strategies for a Linguistically Diverse Classroom	37
	Academic Language Learning Strategies	37
	Vocabulary Building	38
	Reading and Writing Strategies	43
	Summary	48
	Works Cited	49
4	Context: Creating Chief Education Officers (CEOs)	51
	Planning Professional Development that Impacts Instruction and Learning	53
	Professional Development and Levels of Implementation	55
	Professional Development and Sustainability	56
	Booking Agent vs. CEO	57
	CEO and School Change	58
	Principal as CEO	60
	School-University Partnerships	61
	Partnering for School Change	63
	Characteristics of Effective School-University Partnerships	64
	Summary	67
	Works Cited	67
5	Implementing Sustainable Professional Development	69
	Phase One: Preparation and Planning	73
	Collaborate with Experts of ALL and Professional Development	73
	Select CEO Team Participants	75
	Clarify Professional Development Outcomes	78
	Organize Monthly Expectations	84
	Phase Two: Implementation and Reflection	84
	Phase Three: Capacity Building	89
	Authors' Note	89

CONTENTS ix

	Summary	90
	Works Cited	90
6	Visualizing Change	92
	Project CEO Summary	93
	Participants and Professional Development: Tyrrell County	93
	Professional Development Flexibility	95
	Unexpected Favorable Outcomes	96
	Accomplishments and Outcomes	96
	Teachers' Voices	98
	Students' Voices	105
	Principals' Voices	108
	Summary	109
	Authors' Note	110
	Works Cited	110

PREFACE

The inspiration for this book is the positive and powerful change in teacher practice, teacher and principal leadership, and student engagement seen through seven years of delivering professional development in academic language and instructional coaching. It seems irresponsible not to share the experience and what stakeholders have gained in a manner that other professionals can replicate.

The authors have worked collaboratively, delivering professional development in rural eastern North Carolina for seven years. Their initial work involved training the Sheltered Instruction Observation Protocol (SIOP®) (Echevarria, Vogt, and Short 2008) model in school districts with high numbers of English language learners (ELLs). The SIOP® model is a content-based model originally designed to provide effective language instruction so that students can simultaneously access the curriculum while acquiring their second language (L2)—English. Through that work, the authors became aware of the value of academic language literacy for all mainstream classrooms—not just ELLs. Mainstream teachers were sharing that these strategies were helping not only their ELLs but also their special needs students and their native English–speaking students.

The authors had an epiphany that academic language proficiency was more similar to a second language (L2) and therefore this L2 needed to be taught to all students regardless of their native language or their dialect. It was also noted that teachers saw themselves as content specialists and taught the content but were not teaching students how to use academic language as a vehicle for learning the content deeply and more meaningfully.

As the authors continued with their professional development work, they noted that content area teachers were very unaware of what constituted academic language literacy beyond their content-specific vocabulary. Once teachers and students engaged in strategies that taught the content through academic language learning there was a transformation in teaching and learning. This is the story shared with this book for all classroom teachers and principals not just English as a second language (ESL) teachers.

Typically mainstream classroom teachers and principals do not purchase books solely on academic language proficiency because they see these books as the domain of the ESL teacher. We wrote this book so that the school administrators and teachers could have a resource to follow when teaching their content by focusing on academic language. The model and examples are written for mainstream classrooms for immediate implementation.

The book explains the importance of academic language literacy (ALL), gives the reader the skills to identify ALL, describes the steps on how a school can implement ALL via professional development, and outlines an implementation process. This book provides research, rationale, and many strategies for integrating ALL in all content areas. Strategies include both teaching and learning strategies that promote academic language literacy and student-centered approaches.

Professional learning communities have become the norm for professional development in schools. The model presented in this book is easily applicable to the work of professional learning communities. This book describes professional development that takes into account three core elements (content, context, and process) that make for successful professional development and high academic success.

The goal of this book is to provide a "how to" guide with practical examples to both administrators and classroom teachers about capitalizing on professional development that takes into account the context of their school. This book describes and provides examples of effective professional interactions that need to be present for school change. This book describes a job-embedded professional development model that involved peer coaching, teacher-led instructional conversations, and peer observations. Additionally, the book shows how to create a sustainable model.

Another goal of this book is to develop instructional leadership skills of principals and teachers, transforming them from acting as a "booking agent" of professional development to becoming a "chief education officer (CEO)" of instruction and learning. Therefore this book helps instructional leaders by providing an easy-to-follow framework to provide opportunities for professional learning and implementation at their schools. Teachers and administrators must collaborate in changing the pedagogical philosophy to include a focus on academic language literacy. This book shows how this has been done and how the process can be replicated at different schools.

With this book we hope to help teachers learn and implement academic language strategies that help address literacy in their academic fields while they teach their content. K–12 teachers do not see themselves as literacy teachers; they see themselves as content teachers. Teachers alone do not have the time, resources, or authority to learn academic language strategies and to implement them. It is essential that the instructional leader of a school (CEO)—the principal—facilitate this process.

By reading this book we hope that the reader will be able to:

1. Explain and clarify the term academic language literacy (ALL);
2. Incorporate ALL in all classrooms across all content areas;
3. Engage in a professional development process that develops teacher leaders;
4. Describe collaborative models that promote engagement for both teachers and students; and
5. Understand the evolution of the role of the principal from "booking agent" to a "chief education officer, CEO."

WHO MAY USE THIS BOOK?

The intended audiences of this book are professional development directors, principals, and teachers who are looking for innovative practices that result in academic success. This book provides strategies for educators to use when building students' background knowledge and growing students' academic language necessary for success in school. These students have been defined as standard English learners (SELs) and require the targeted language instruction that this book promotes.

RESEARCH BASIS

The research basis for this book comes from three areas of research that are fully researched and developed in their fields yet not integrated as this book attempts to do. The three research areas are professional development, academic language literacy, and instructional leadership. Professional development research permeates throughout the book by promoting strategies and techniques that facilitate job-embedded coaching and reflection by teachers through the leadership of the principal.

Language acquisition strategies proven to be effective among ELLs to learn English have proven in our research to be effective in learning academic language. The research on academic language literacy is the basis of the strategies presented for learning academic language in the mainstream classroom. The third area of research presented in this book is on the principal as instructional leader. In our research in the past seven years it has been demonstrated time and time again that only if the principal is invested in the professional development will there be a change in teacher practice.

The focus on academic language literacy is the equalizer in this book. By focusing on listening, speaking, reading, and writing academic language, principals are able to apply the principles of professional development and facilitate change in instruction that not only improves instruction but also develops teacher leaders.

WORKS CITED

Chamot, Anna Uhl, and J. Michael O'Malley. *The CALLA Handbook: Implementing the Cognitive Academic Language Learning Approach*. Boston: Addison-Wesley, 1994.

Echevarria, Jana, MaryEllen Vogt, and Deborah Short. *Making Content Comprehensible for English Language Learners: The SIOP Model*. 3rd Edition. Boston: Pearson Education, 2008.

Marzano, Robert. *Building Background Knowledge for Academic Achievement: Research on What Works in Schools*. Alexandria: Association of Supervision and Curriculum Development, 2004.

O'Neal, Debra, and Marjorie Ringler. "Broadening our View of Linguistic Diversity." *Phi Delta Kappan* 91.7 (2010): 48–52.

EFFECTIVE PROFESSIONAL DEVELOPMENT

A Three-Pronged Approach

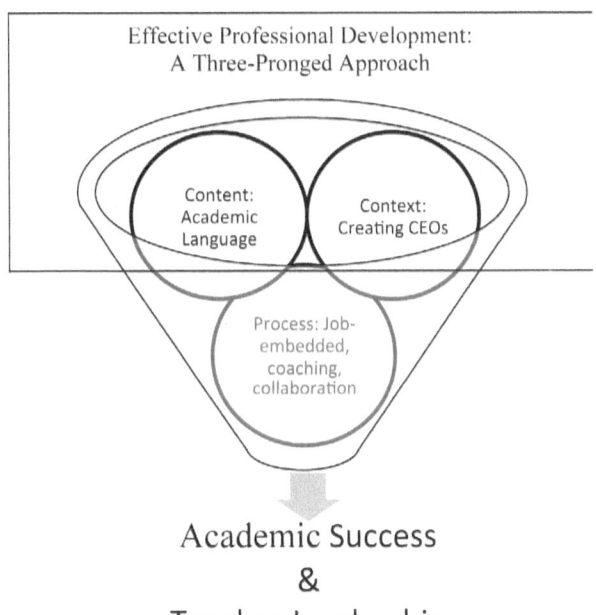

Chapter 1 Organizer

Effective professional development that results in student academic success and teacher leadership is three-dimensional. The three dimensions: content, context, and process are essential to professional development.

Content is the "what" to be learned and implemented. The content of any professional development should be research-based and appropriate to promote students' success.

Delivering content alone devoid of understanding the context misses the aspect of relevancy to the audience. A professional developer must understand the "who" or audience as well as the context to provide examples and strategies that will be useful to a specific site. Finally, the "what" and the "who" need to be taught using an effective process. The "how" from introduction to follow-up is essential to developing instructional leadership skills.

The next sections describe each of the three prongs necessary for professional development to result in developing and improving principals' instructional leadership skills and teachers' practice all by focusing on academic language.

CONTENT: ACADEMIC LANGUAGE MATTERS

Academic language is nobody's native language. English speakers who speak regional variations of English and dialects do not enter school speaking the language of textbooks. More so, English language learners (ELLs) sit in classrooms trying to learn the content while they struggle to understand English. The content of the K–12 curriculum has a strong literacy component. Curriculum of each content area, predominately written material, is found in content standards, books, websites, and curriculum kits. This material is written in standard academic English and therefore academic language matters!

Many states have adopted the Common Core State Standards (CCSS) that specifically focus on learning from informational texts. In addition, English Language Arts (ELA) CCSS provide an integrated view of the areas within the language arts: reading, writing, speaking/listening, and language. For this reason it is important to focus on academic language literacy (ALL). Curriculum standards, including the CCSS, have a strong emphasis on reading, writing, and comprehension. For teachers, it is a daunting job to integrate CCSS and ALL in their already busy workday. For this reason, the next section explains language literacy in order to understand the content of ALL.

Conventions of Standard English

A student who is achieving academically is expected to demonstrate command of standard academic English when speaking and writing. In order to do so, the student must demonstrate command of the conventions of standard academic written English such as correct punctuation and grammar in addition to vocabulary. Oftentimes, teachers will accept students' written work and oral responses that are not written in academic language because the content is accurate. This practice will not meet the curriculum standard of the twenty-first century.

In this day and age, for students to achieve academically it is expected that they use appropriate academic language and the conventions of standard English to convey their knowledge of the academic content. Students need to have knowledge of language because there are different conventions of language used in different contexts. For example, the academic language and conventions of standard English used in a science report are different from that of a persuasive essay or that of a mathematical rationale for solving a problem. Students who understand language are able to make effective choices for meaning and style.

Teachers and administrators in their preparation programs are taught in the same manner K–12 students are taught in that they learn the content of their field. Teachers learn how to write lesson plans and teach lessons. Administrators are taught how to lead schools and how to facilitate school environments conducive to learning. The focus is on how to become a practitioner and the emphasis on language is not typically included in their learning. For this reason, professional development is an essential tool for teachers and administrators to continually engage in professional learning to improve their roles.

Again, professional development for educators typically focuses on how to improve teaching; therefore, professional development that provides tools to integrate content and academic language proficiency is essential. Fillmore and Fillmore explain that for those who are proficient in academic language and can read texts, professional articles, and even policy, language is invisible; however, for someone who is not academic language proficient, reading complex texts, professional articles, or any standard English material becomes difficult because language becomes a huge barrier that prevents learning. Teachers and administrators are not experts in ALL and therefore professional development that helps facilitate teachers' learning of language in the content area is important.

One such professional development that helps integrate academic language and content is the Sheltered Instruction Observation Protocol (SIOP®) (Echevarria, Vogt, and Short 2008). This is a content-based instructional model that is typically used by ESL teachers. In the authors' research and experience, when the SIOP® model is implemented with fidelity in the mainstream classroom, the model becomes a tool for both teachers and students to integrate academic language instruction and content learning. There are other content-based instruction models such as the CHATS Model (Himmele and Himmele 2009), and Six Steps to Vocabulary Development (Marzano 2009). In this book the authors utilize portions of the SIOP® model because it is the model used in the research for this book. This model is explained in detail in chapter 2.

Features of Academic Language

Understanding the conventions of standard English is necessary; however, administrators, teachers, and students need to also understand and use academic language for academic success. The discussion in this section continues with a brief description of the features of academic language and their importance for academic success. Academic language is much more than the vocabulary of the content. There are several features of academic language (Zwiers 2008):

Feature 1. Academic language is used to describe complexity. In other words, academic language is used to describe complex concepts as clearly as possible.

Feature 2. Academic language is used to describe higher-order thinking. In other words, academic language and the complex processes in feature 1 are used to comprehend, solve problems, and express ideas.

Feature 3. Academic language is used to describe abstractions. In other words, language is more than just simple sentences; language is used in complex sentences, for example, "On the other hand, the two scientists had differing views on the topic." For students who have only a basic understanding of language, their interpretation of this sentence is a concrete interpretation, and when you read the sentence for literal meaning this sentence makes no sense! An academic language proficient student is able to understand the conventions of the language in the written sentence and make meaningful sense of what the sentence is conveying.

Feature 4. Academic language proficiency helps students understand and use figurative expressions. Students who are proficient in academic language have no problems understanding expressions such as "boils down to," "sidestep an issue," "read between the lines," "outweigh," "the answer does not hold water," "the elephant in the room," "set the stage for." Imagine what a student thinks if their academic language is deficient—the fall back in language development is a literal meaning!

Feature 5. Academic language used in texts is written for a distant audience. Language in texts is explicit because authors assume that they need to clearly explain all details for the reader to understand. Students need to learn this skill when they write in their content classes. By conveying their responses in class, students need to learn to avoid vague pronouns and be explicit in their responses. By doing so, teachers will know that the student is fluent in the language of the content and thus knows the content.

Feature 6. Academic language often uses nominalization. Nominalization is the making of verbs or adjectives into nouns and noun phrases. For example, one may find this type of sentence in complex texts: "The resolution on usage of academic language in the classroom led to rebellion from the teachers." In this case the words *resolve*, *use*, and *rebel* are used as nouns. Again, for a student who is not proficient in academic language, these words are written differently and because they are not looking at the sentence with a focus on language they will stop at the words and throw up their hands in frustration. If the student is focused on language, then the student may use a strategy of looking at the root of a word and make connections for meaning.

A classroom that focuses on academic language proficiency will explicitly teach language strategies, whereas a typical classroom not focusing on language will struggle with learning due to the academic language barriers.

So What Is Academic Language?

Academic language is the language necessary for success in school: the language of printed text. There are many components of academic language. This book focuses on three: process and function words, complex morphology, and content-specific vocabulary.

Process and function words are words not specific to content areas. Examples of process words: justify, explain, list, compare, contrast, define, analyze, persuade. Examples of transition words: therefore, however, in conclusion. Examples of sequence words: first, then, finally. What does this mean instructionally? Teachers must teach students how to perform the functions and processes. Additionally, teachers and students become aware of the various ways to interpret these words according to the different content areas.

Morphology of words helps make meaning of unfamiliar words by using morphemes. One such morpheme: roots. Academic language contains roots that come from Greek and Latin languages. Here is a tidbit of information that may show the value of taking the time to teach roots as part of content instruction: Fourteen roots provide the meaning for over 100,000 words! Here is an example: Unreliable contains the roots rely and able. By stopping to point out the roots, teachers are opening their students' eyes to focus on language and to make meaning by using academic language strategies.

Teachers can teach content by teaching about other morphemes in addition to teaching about roots. A morpheme is the smallest unit of meaning (e.g., "s" = plural). By pointing out to students how morphemes influence the meaning of a word, they help students gather meaning from unfamiliar words as well. Chapter 2 discusses academic language in more detail.

Content-specific vocabulary needs to be taught using language strategies for meaningful learning instead of useless lists that are memorized for the test and then forgotten. It is important to identify the morphology of content-specific and complex words. The reason this book is important is that it helps school administrators and teachers maintain focus on language strategies to help improve instruction. Teachers don't typically plan to use language strategies to teach the content. This book provides a rationale of the importance of developing academic language in teaching and learning.

In addition, this book provides strategies and examples for teachers to incorporate these strategies in their teaching. Teachers must *expect* students to use academic language when they speak and write. In order to do so, it is important to scaffold for academic language use by utilizing language strategies such as: Use sentence frames in speaking and in writing, use morphology, develop academic vocabulary, enhance academic writing across content areas, use note-taking skills, and use graphic organizers. Most importantly, teachers and administrators must model the use of academic language for students to see, hear, and read.

One strategy effective in implementing language strategies is writing language objectives that identify language structures needed for a lesson. Language objectives should complement the content objective of a lesson. Language objectives are described in more detail in chapter 2 with a more in-depth discussion about the content (the "what") of ALL professional development. The next section provides a description of the context (the "who") of professional development.

CONTEXT: CREATING CHIEF EDUCATION OFFICERS (CEOs)

The role of the principal is to provide organizational support that facilitates implementation of academic language literacy in content areas. This role is defined in this book as the essence of a chief education officer (CEO). A CEO's role is different from that of the traditional "booking agent" of professional development. This book helps principals understand the importance of the role of a CEO that improves academic achievement by focusing on ALL.

This book provides a principal with tools that engage him or her in professional development of teachers. This is very different from what principals normally do: book the presenter, book the room, purchase materials, purchase snacks, introduce the speaker, and then leave the room to take care of other duties. In this book, the principal provides organizational support by participating in the professional development, providing feedback, teaching teachers how to provide peer feedback, learning from challenges, and celebrating successes.

In the many years that the authors have delivered professional development, teachers and principals realized that broadening the focus of teaching content to include ALL made sense. The professional development research shared in this book was conducted in rural areas of eastern North Carolina. The authors initially delivered professional development in the SIOP® model, originally intended for ELLs. Each time SIOP® professional development ended the authors and participants came to the realization that student learning improved not just for ELLs but also for native English–speaking learners.

Teachers and students also realized that they had strong dialectal variations of English, typically southern English variations, that impacted student learning. This realization led to a broadened focus of professional development about academic language in the various districts in rural eastern North Carolina. This broadened focus on ALL was well received and instructional leadership skills for principals and teachers improved.

In addition to broadening the focus on ALL, it became evident that successful districts had engaged principals, engaged district-level administrators, and a follow-up professional development plan in place. The unsuccessful schools had "booking agents," principals who booked the session, left for the day, and had no follow-up activities planned. The goal of this book is to provide a guide to CEOs for successful implementation of ALL strategies.

Am I a CEO or Do I Need to Work on This?

Early in the authors' collaboration with schools, two principals at two elementary schools within the same school district modeled CEO behaviors. The two principals realized that in order for professional development to be effective they needed to be involved at all levels of implementation. The principals attended the initial two-and-a-half-day workshop, facilitated joint monthly meetings, and supported their teachers through meaningful instructional conversations centered on the use of academic language strategies and the SIOP® (explained in more detail in chapter 2).

Unfortunately, these two principals were unique examples of CEOs. More often principals are booking agents and unless professional developers insist on a high level of involvement from principals and teachers, the leadership does not engage in ongoing professional development and thus teachers are not likely to implement strategies in their lessons.

As time passed, the authors of this book decided to deliver training only in school districts that engaged in ongoing follow-up activities. The type of ongoing follow-up activities varied; some school districts partnered with the authors to deliver follow-up activities, and others worked with the authors to plan follow-up activities and then the school principal facilitated the activities. Follow-up activities should be ongoing with job-embedded support.

After many years of working with CEOs and booking agents, the authors arrived at the conclusion that principals who were engaged in teachers' implementation improved their instructional leadership skills, facilitated improvement in teaching, and developed teacher leaders. Principals who booked professional developers to deliver training and did not carefully plan ongoing efforts to support implementation did not show change in teaching practices. This "epiphany" led the authors to write a grant "Project CEO: Chief Education Officer," which was funded by NC Quest, a sub-award from the Department of Education. Project CEO was based on these two core beliefs:

- High-quality professional development starts with the principal
- The principal must be part of the process, *not* just a facilitator

Project CEO outlined ongoing job-embedded professional development based on these core activities: peer coaching, use of academic language, and professional reflection. The core activities were only possible in schools where principals engaged in the process and where participants saw the value in the content of the professional development and therefore were willing to take risks by trying strategies with lots of support.

The role of the CEO is described in more detail in chapter 4; therefore a brief discussion in this paragraph will help understand the gist of what it means to be a CEO. The CEO works with teachers meaningfully as part of a team. It is important that the expectations of the team be clearly stated. In order for professional development to be implemented in classrooms it is important to have ongoing monthly expectations and activities that align with these expectations. The first, and most important, expectation is that ALL strategies be implemented daily in classrooms.

ALL strategies should be implemented incrementally, allowing for time to learn and practice using new strategies on a monthly basis. For example, during the first month of implementation it is important to include language objectives along with the content objectives; therefore, teachers add a place in their lesson plans to write language objectives. The most important part is that the team studies and discusses language objectives in order to get a good understanding of what these objectives are.

CEOs would take language objectives a step further and expect teachers to write objectives in student-friendly language because there is an expectation that the objectives be used with students and by students. Project CEO changed the old practice of writing objectives in language of standards because principals and teachers quickly agreed that using the language of the standards meant that the objectives were written for administrative purposes and ultimately was not relevant to students and to what students thought they were learning.

A second important expectation of a CEO is that teachers engage in peer coaching. This practice is the most difficult to facilitate yet the most important. Teachers learn best from each other and in order to learn from each other they should have the opportunity to practice and get feedback on their practice. Peer coaching is not common practice; therefore the CEO should show teachers how to observe and provide feedback. The authors in their research have found that teachers who engaged in peer observations and coaching were successful in implementing professional development. Many of them also became teacher leaders in their schools!

A third important expectation of a CEO is to provide opportunities for teachers to engage in reflection. Reflecting with peers, individually, and with their principal is beneficial to improving teaching. An effective CEO develops trusting and caring relationships and therefore teachers feel comfortable engaging in instructional dialogue with their principals.

In the authors' research it was found that teachers who regarded their principals as CEOs valued the feedback and instructional conversation higher than receiving resources or additional time for planning. Teachers who regarded their principals as CEOs explained that it was important to know that their principals understood the challenges they were facing and the demands on their time. It made it easier for teachers to discuss challenges, and more importantly, offer solutions!

A principal's presence and engagement are worth more than money. Principals who become CEOs change their relationship with teachers. Professional relationships become deeper and more meaningful in the improvement of teaching and student learning.

The final expectation of CEOs is to value learning and always engage teachers in learning. In the authors' research, CEO principals engaged teachers in learning opportunities at every interaction. Many principals work through professional learning communities in many ways. One big criticism authors often hear from teachers is that the learning communities take on too many projects. A CEO should prioritize the initiatives that teachers and schools should engage in and always try to integrate initiatives instead of maintaining initiatives as separate activities. If the initiatives do not integrate, it is important to have a discussion with teachers and decide which initiatives to keep, delete, or add.

In this book a case is made to make the implementation of ALL strategies a priority. This book shows how these strategies can become part of most instructional models of a school. The key is for the CEOs to engage teachers in learning; therefore the learning opportunities in school need to be well organized. Monthly reading of journal articles, discussions of implementation successes and challenges, and ongoing implementation of strategies has proven to be successful ways to increase ALL among students.

In summary, CEOs engage in educational coaching, their students are their teachers, and their classroom is the entire building. Every exchange with a teacher is an opportunity to teach about ALL and thus improve teaching. CEOs engage in a learning process with their teachers where they explore, critique, reflect, and transform practice. This process is unique and different at each school because teachers have unique personalities and different professional experiences. The key is *trust*. The CEO and teachers trust each other and have a common goal to create positive change in teaching and learning by focusing on ALL of students. Engaging in a collaborative process that relies heavily on job-embedded coaching strengthens this trust.

In addition to relationships, CEOs need to be efficient; thus, later the book discusses and provides samples of helpful documents such as peer observation questions, observation forms, coaching reflection templates, and reading reflection templates. This book also shares how the authors used technology to help facilitate communication among teams of CEOs and teachers.

PROCESS: JOB-EMBEDDED COACHING AND COLLABORATION

Now that the content, academic language, and the context, role of the CEO, have been explained, it is time to discuss the process of embedding coaching and collaboration within the teachers' daily work. Next to understanding "what" and "who" is facilitating this learning is the "how" to teach academic language. The process described in this book is based on seven years of applying this process and tweaking it along the way. Remember that each school is unique and so the process presented is generic so that CEOs can tailor it to their schools.

Building capacity of teacher leaders who are able to translate the professional development strategies into practice, resulting in improved teaching and student learning, is a three-phase process: preparation and planning, implementation and reflection, and capacity building.

Phase One: Preparation and Planning

The CEO of a school is the principal; however, the principal does not teach students directly. For this reason the principal and a team of teachers should work together as a CEO team. The first phase is for the CEO team to learn an ALL model (see chapter 2 for the various models) and to become competent in the systemic application of ALL strategies. The CEO team needs time to learn the model and to fully integrate academic language and content-area instruction; therefore, this initial phase of professional development should establish the protocols and procedures for the yearlong job-embedded coaching and collaboration.

Phase Two: Implementation and Reflection

In this phase, CEO teams collaborate to apply their ALL knowledge throughout the school year and provide each other feedback through coaching and learning communities. A sample yearlong professional structure is listed in table 1.1. In Project CEO, teams met with the authors of this book three times each month—essentially once a week, leaving the final week for the authors to analyze data, use data to gauge level of implementation, and plan activities for the next month. During these three monthly meetings, CEO team members modeled coaching strategies while practicing observations (both live and video recorded), engaged in study groups, and gave and received peer feedback, allowing for the implementation of the ALL strategies.

It is important to continue learning during the yearlong process. One strategy that worked in this project was the monthly reading of journal articles and book discussions. The CEO team read the text "Academic Language for English Language Learners and Struggling Readers" (Freeman and Freeman 2009) as well as carefully selected articles on the topic of the month. During this phase the CEO team allocated time during monthly meetings to create supplementary materials such as manipulatives, crafts, and graphic organizers useful in making content instruction more comprehensible for students.

Reflection. As part of phase two academic year activities, the CEO team reflects on the impact of implementation on classroom instruction. Using the data collected in phases one and two, the CEO team develops their own professional development, typically during the summer months, to train

Table 1.1. Sample Phase Activities

Phase One: Preparation and Planning March–July	The CEO team decides on: • materials to focus on for coaching • pre/post-assessments and various assessment instruments • baseline data on coaching and ALL • pre-assessment data • professional development materials for monthly coaching
Phase Two: Implementation and Reflection August–June	• Monthly professional development in ALL • Weekly observations, feedback, coaching, and professional learning communities (PLC)s • Monthly reflection activities about learning and implementation
Phase Two: Reflection June–July	• CEO team writes training and coaching plans for next year's professional development to be delivered to all faculty and staff • ALL/Professional development experts coach CEO team while writing their own professional development
Phase Three: Capacity Building August–June	• CEO team delivers training to all faculty and staff • Monthly peer coaching • Monthly professional development in ALL • Weekly observations, feedback, coaching, and PLCs • Repeat reflection activities from phase two

their entire school faculty. In Project CEO, the authors provided coaching and mentoring during this phase. The CEO team delivered the training developed prior to the beginning of phase three.

Phase Three: Capacity Building

The CEO team delivers professional development they wrote based on their learning and implementation. The CEO team replicates the learning activities they experienced the previous year. The difference this time is that the CEO team's teacher leaders facilitate the yearlong professional learning in collaboration with the principal.

Additional activities highly recommended but not required include attendance to national conferences on the topic of ALL. Project CEO was able to take four teachers to the international conference of Teachers of English to Students of Other Languages (TESOL). This experience was valuable because it was the first time that these teachers had attended such a large conference—20,000 attendees. For two of the teachers it was the first time they had flown in an airplane.

At the TESOL conference the authors selected the conference sessions to attend because of their familiarity with the topic and expertise in ALL. Project CEO teachers and the authors not only learned at each session but also engaged teachers back home by keeping them updated about new content and experiences. Project CEO teachers also had the opportunity to have lunch with the two authors, whose book they read and whose ideas and strategies were implemented in their classrooms.

SUMMARY

It is important to account for the content, context, and process in the implementation of professional development, especially when implementing academic language strategies in lessons. The success of the implementation is highly influenced by the leadership approach exhibited by the principal. Principals who engage in the process and meet every challenge openly, honestly, and collaboratively with their teachers will have success in implementation. Academic language matters in the education of children. Administrators and teachers have the responsibility of teaching academic language in order to prepare students to listen, speak, read, and write in the language of academic success. The next chapter defines more deeply what this book means by academic language.

WORKS CITED

Echevarria, Jana, MaryEllen Vogt, and Deborah Short. *Making Content Comprehensible for English Language Learners: The SIOP Model.* 3rd Edition. Boston: Pearson Education, 2008.

Fillmore, Lily Wong, and Charles J. Fillmore. "Text Complexity, Common Core, and ELLs." *Understanding Language.* https://www.youtube.com/watch?v=STFTX7UiBz0. Berkeley: Stanford University, 2012.

Freeman, Yvonne, and David Freeman. *Academic Language for English Language Learners and Struggling Readers: How to Help Students Succeed Across the Content Areas.* Portsmouth: Heinemann, 2009.

Himmele, Persida, and William Himmele. *The Language Rich Classroom: A Research Based Framework for Teaching English Language Learners.* 2nd Edition. Alexandria: Association for Supervision and Curriculum Development, 2009.

Marzano, Robert J. "Six Steps to Better Vocabulary Instruction." *Educational Leadership* 67.1 (2009): 83–84.

Zwiers, Jeff. *Building Academic Language: Essential Practices for Content Classrooms.* Hoboken: Wiley, 2008.

2

CONTENT

What Comprises Academic Language Literacy (ALL)?

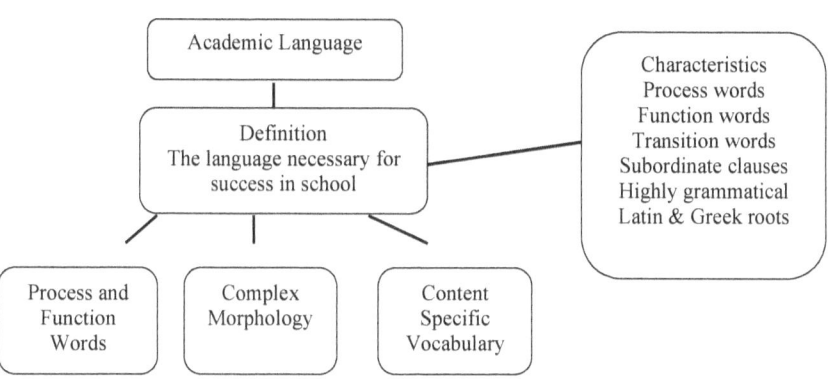

Chapter 2 Organizer

Ask any teacher or any non-linguist to define academic language and the answer will likely be that it is grammatically correct, slang-free language. Although that is an accurate piece of the picture, it is not the whole picture. Academic language is essentially the register or variety of language necessary for success in school. Without it, students cannot access the curriculum through the texts or lectures, nor can they appropriately write about or speak about the course content. As Corson clarifies, academic language serves as a gatekeeper barring entry to higher levels of education to those who do not achieve fluency (1997, 675). He refers to academic language as the "meta-language" that is used to talk about text, whether in conversation or in written form.

Cummins's seminal work in 1984 in the field of linguistics created the acronyms BICS (Basic Interpersonal Communication Skills) and CALP (Cognitive Academic Language Proficiency), which are still frequently referred to today. BICS is commonly regarded as "social language" or everyday language and CALP is considered "academic language." In 1994, Chamot and O'Malley elaborated on Cummins's distinction between BICS and CALP. They concurred that academic language is de-contextualized and differs greatly from social language, which often takes place in face-to-face communication accompanied with body language, variations in tone, and concrete clues to aid comprehension. They claim that while academic language is limited in context clues, this is only one of the issues that learners confront.

Goldenberg and Coleman reiterate that knowing the difference between academic and everyday language is essential for effective academic instruction (2010, 61). They further remind us that academic language instruction should not be limited to just the vocabulary of the content subjects. Additionally, they found that teachers *erroneously* believed that mere exposure to a language-rich environment at school would yield acquisition of language proficiency (Goldenberg and Coleman 2010, 64). To the contrary, teachers need to teach the complexities of academic language and its components: *process/function words* as well as the *complex morphology* and *content-specific language*.

In the authors' work with hundreds of classroom teachers over the years, teachers are asked to create a T-Chart which compared the characteristics of social language to those of academic language. Table 2.1 provides a sample T-Chart developed by a group of teachers. Time and again the focus they provide is limited to slang, texting language, and lack of grammaticality. The authors often have to introduce the idea of content vocabulary, grammatical structures, and process words. The teachers contend that they would know academic language when they encounter it, but they are unaware that they do little to promote it.

The authors became keenly aware that it is impossible to expect teachers to teach academic language if they neither use it themselves nor are able to identify it. After a year of working with an elementary and middle school on a weekly basis, teachers confessed that at the outset they thought they knew what academic language was, but now they can honestly say they were mistaken. Their original understanding of academic language was very superficial and based on content vocabulary alone, but now they

Table 2.1. Sample T-Chart Comparing Social Language and Academic Language

Social Language	Academic Language
Slang	Content vocabulary
Simple sentence structure	Complex sentence structure
Vague	Language of textbooks
Dialect	Standard English
Conversational	Often in written form (reports, research papers, journal articles)
Language used in playground	Language used in content classrooms, used to convey higher-order thinking

have a broader, deeper comprehension of the many facets to truly using and teaching academic language, which in turn will yield academic success.

If academic language is indeed a second language for all students, it is, therefore, native to no one; it is not learned in the home, and must be taught in school. How teachers unfamiliar with language teaching strategies accomplish this goal is addressed in this chapter. Taking from the ESL field where it is necessary to teach both language and content effectively, this chapter explores the strategy of content-based instruction (CBI).

COMPONENTS OF ACADEMIC LANGUAGE

There are many components of academic language. The three components discussed in this section (process/function words, morphology, and content-specific vocabulary) have been part of the authors' professional development and research that have demonstrated a positive change in instruction and students' academic language proficiency.

Process/Function Words

In the classroom, students are often asked to perform academic activities that require process and function words. Chamot and O'Malley created a list that shows how these words are necessary for success in all classes; the list is not specific to one content area; for example: list, justify, explain, compare/contrast, define, analyze, persuade, evaluate, assess, predict, and identify. The list is quite extensive, but the point to be taken is that in daily social conversations one rarely would say, "Can you compare and contrast the various options available to you?" No, one doesn't, but in the classroom a student will be asked to compare and contrast or to explain or justify why a specific event occurred and to give support to the statement. Teachers have to look at the different academic activities that are asked of students, but additionally, teachers need to examine the language with which they are being asked to perform these skills.

A child may be asked to analyze a poem, analyze a math equation, analyze the series of events that led to a war, or analyze the results of a science experiment. In each of these contexts, the process of analysis may be accomplished differently, may be orally explained differently, and may be written differently, yet the word used to ask the question is the same. Students need direct instruction in these process words that do not occur in their daily social interactions. In social language, one would just be asked the question *why*, but analysis requires a specific skill set that can only be learned through direct context-based classroom instruction.

Classrooms are often places where these types of process words are being replaced by the more comprehensible social version in order for the students to process the content; however, the high-stakes tests they take are using the academic language. When the student is unsuccessful in school or in testing, often blame falls on the student for not knowing the content, yet it is often the language that is the barrier (Bielenberg and Fillmore 2004, 45).

In discussions with classroom teachers the authors were told that the students knew the content well, they did everything correctly in class, but then did poorly on the standardized test. Upon further examination, it was revealed that the language of the test was different from the language being used to explain, teach, and review the concepts in the classroom. To further emphasize this with the teachers involved in the authors' study, teachers were asked to look at their end of the grade tests with their students and to analyze each question on old tests.

Students were asked to circle or highlight the language of the test that would give them trouble or make it difficult to understand the question. Through this process it became even clearer to both the teachers and the students how important it was to learn the academic language along with the content.

Morphology

Morphology is the linguistic study of morphemes, or the smallest unit of meaning in a word. It is often difficult for mainstream teachers to look at language as if they were linguists because they are trained to be content specialists. However, all content is taught using language and by ignoring the morphological component of language development, teachers miss numerous opportunities to grow their students' vocabulary.

So what is morphology in a nutshell? Any component of a word that carries meaning is a morpheme. For example: bird**s**—the **s** means plural and is, therefore, a morpheme. In the sentence: The bird**'s** beak was orange, the **'s** takes on the meaning of possessive and, therefore, carries meaning. All prefixes and suffixes are morphemes, as are roots.

So how does the study of morphology benefit students in a way that helps grow their vocabulary and understanding of academic language? For starters, by analyzing words in context students can often decipher meaning based on the morphology. Teachers can also make these "morphology moments" into teachable moments that carry across the curriculum. A great example of this is the use of the word *audience* in the language arts classroom. Students are told to read aloud for the *audience*; a teacher who is cued into morphology may stop the class and analyze the word *audience*. The class excitedly brainstorms as many words that contain the same root *audi* (to hear) and may come up with a list that includes auditorium and audiobook. But did they come up with auditory? Did they know that an audience can be an abstract concept or that an auditorium has broader meaning than the school auditorium? Do they see the connection with auditorium, audience, and auditory?

These "morphology moments" can lead to discussions that will not only enhance their understanding of language, but will make them better students in other content areas. When the teachers realize that teaching language is not the sole domain of the language arts or English teacher, they will truly begin achieving academic language literacy for all students.

Along with morphology, teachers should teach the concept of homonyms, homophones, and homographs. Homonyms are usually taught as a broad concept that is understood to be two words that sound alike, but have different meanings. When one looks at it more closely, there is a benefit by breaking this into three more specific categories: homonyms, homophones, and homographs. Looking at the morphology of these three words: homo- means same, -nym means name, -phone means sound, and -graph means writing or spelling. This, therefore, produces three types of words:

Homonyms: words that are *spelled alike* and *sound alike*, BUT mean different things.

Homophones: words that *sound alike*, but are *spelled differently* AND mean different things.

Homograph: words that are *spelled alike*, BUT *sound different* and mean different things

Table 2.2. Sample Homonyms, Homophones, and Homographs

Homonyms	Homophones	Homographs
Pupil (student)	Heard (past tense hear)	Wind (weather)
Pupil (eye)	Herd (group of cattle)	Wind (turn a handle)
Compact (small)	Read (read a book)	Bow (for your hair)
Compact (agreement)	Reed (vegetation)	Bow (show respect)

Examples of homonyms, homophones, and homographs are shown in table 2.2.

By introducing the linguistic concept of homonyms, homophones, and homographs, teachers instantly help students develop language awareness and increase their vocabularies. As the authors worked with teachers, the authors saw classrooms that created lists for these word categories and teachers would stop a lesson whenever a student heard a homonym, homophone, or homograph being used. The word was discussed and then the class made a decision as to which category the new word pair belonged.

A perfect example of awareness of homonyms, homophones, and homographs was a class that was discussing electricity and the parts of the light bulb. The teacher was showing a light bulb and talked about the various conductors and how electricity travels. The authors' minds instantly went to the image of a train conductor, which had the authors stop the teacher, and curiously asked if this was the same thing. The students told the authors that it was not, while someone else mentioned a conductor directs an orchestra. At this teachable moment the class decided that conductor/conductor/conductor were homonyms because all three are spelled alike and sound alike but mean different things.

In the conductor example a new trio of words was added to the homonym chart. This little detour from the lesson took all of two minutes, but exposed children to new words and linguistic concepts in a meaningful context. Given the various backgrounds of the children in classrooms, it is possible that someone in the class was also wondering what the train conductor or musical conductor had to do with light bulbs!

Content-Specific Vocabulary

In 2000, Coxhead developed the academic word list that looked at a large corpus of texts that shows the complexity of the words that frequently appear in academic texts (232). Marzano addresses word frequency lists and points out that although they clearly tell us how frequently specific words appear in specific types of text, they don't address the importance of such words, nor do they address the appearance of these words across content areas. In spite of the creation of these academic word lists, teachers have been blindly teaching content-specific vocabulary to students already. So what makes the academic word list different from current practice? Coxhead points out the origin of the most frequently occurring academic words is Latin or Greek, while the social language vocabulary is most often of Anglo-Saxon roots (2000, 225).

The academic language often found in classroom texts and complex books is not the language used in daily conversations. It is unfamiliar to all students entering school and is rarely taught at home since it is clearly the language of academics. Academic language includes not only the vocabulary specific to each content area, but the words used to connect text, to indicate what is coming next in the text, and to summarize the text. The process words that direct students to perform a variety of academic tasks are also considered academic language even though they are not specific to one subject area.

It is a true eye-opener for teachers to realize that the process and function words mentioned earlier are also a part of academic language. Often teachers will tell the authors that academic language includes only the vocabulary lists and key content words in their subject matter that students are expected to memorize out of context. These words, although very important to the students' academic success, can only be appropriately used if they are connected by the process/function words and used in the context of specific classroom content.

An example of academic language in use occurred while observing a high school science class. The authors circulated the room to listen as students were recording their observations for their lab reports. The authors had been working with this teacher for a few months and he was struggling with the concept of academic language and how to teach it. However, when the authors were walking by a group of students, a young lady was saying, "the . . . sucked up the color." She then looked at the authors, knowing they were the teachers helping her teacher with the academic language proficiency workshops, and said, "What's the *smart way* to say sucked up?" She was highly aware that her word choice was not acceptable academic language, but was momentarily stumped looking for the correct word. She quickly came up with *absorb* and was so proud. But the most telling piece for the authors was the fact she had learned to differentiate between social language and academic language.

WHO NEEDS ACADEMIC LANGUAGE LITERACY?

Group #1: Native Speakers of English or Standard English Learners (SELs)

As young children prepare to begin kindergarten, the primary language to which they have been exposed is the home language. Although most districts use some form of a "home language survey" to assess English language proficiency or ELL status, none of them look at the dialect of English spoken in the home. The authors of this book contend that the home dialect is equally as important to academic success as the home language.

Linguists consistently define a dialect as a variety of language that is mutually comprehensible by two speakers of the same language. In other words, a New Yorker can understand a North Carolinian, yet their varieties of English are different. All speakers of regional dialects identify closely with their dialect, which leads to the viewpoint that "you are what you speak." According to Wolfram and Shilling-Estes, the language variety used gives a person a sense of identity and place.

Linguists argue that it is difficult to clearly define what constitutes a dialect because often political and geographic boundaries create "languages" that are still mutually intelligible. However, for the sake of definition, dialects are most often identified as being composed of three crucial elements: accent, lexicon, and syntax. In other words, all varieties of English whether regionally, ethnically, or socioeconomically classified have unique accents, a unique vocabulary, and specific grammatical characteristics. Using these characteristics to classify dialects shows that from the perspective of their structural quality, if they possess the three characteristics then they are linguistically all equal.

However, a personal set of values tells that dialects are not equally valued; society values some varieties of language more than others and marginalizes some varieties more than others. Nieto has an even stronger perspective and states that "when particular languages are prohibited or denigrated, the voices of those who speak them are silenced and rejected as well" (2002, 82). This view of languages can be extended to dialects to state that when a particular dialect is denigrated, so are its speakers.

Teachers, often untrained in linguistics, are only trained as traditional prescriptive grammarians. Given this training, they view their role as the "grammar police" to tell students how to read, write, and speak "correctly" (whatever their definition of "correctly" is). Ideally this is an admirable task; however, there are a variety of flaws with this mindset. First, on routine observation in southern schools, the authors have seen teachers raised in the region using the local dialect including its regional syntactical varieties, which would be considered "incorrect" by a prescriptive grammarian. For example: "We *might could* do that when we finish our review." This double modal is completely acceptable in the local variety of English, but unacceptable in both standard and academic English.

A second flaw with a prescriptive mindset is that many varieties of rural southern English and African American Vernacular English (AAVE) are considered prescriptively structurally unacceptable, yet they are the L1 or native language of its speakers. If one returns to the "you are what you speak" mantra, one realizes that correcting a student's native variety and labeling it "incorrect" can be damaging. However, as educators, one knows that teachers must teach both standard English and academic English if one wants to give students the tools for academic and economic success. Freeman and Freeman refer to these students who are native speakers, but not fluent in standard English as Standard English Learners (SELs) (2009, 10). SELs need instruction in academic language in order to achieve academic success.

It is very important to be sensitive to dialectal differences and to extend the same sensitivity to students with language differences. By treating academic language as the target language for all learners (L2), one can still respect the students' native language (L1), whether it is a language or a dialectal variation of English.

With dialects that differ from the standard, teachers need to purposefully teach students what it means to "code switch" or move between different registers of English. These students essentially need to become bidialectal or fluent in both their native dialect and the target language of academic English. Future discussions in this book about academic language literacy will be referring to students who not only speak different languages, but also students who speak a dialect other than standard English. These native speakers will be referred to as SELs.

Group #2: English Language Learners (ELLs)

In Cummins's work (1984) there is a distinction between social (BICS) and academic (CALP) language. Just like native speakers, second-language learners acquire the social forms of language first. Imagine sitting in a classroom with a teacher who is instructing using a direct approach, no visuals, rapid speech, and a vocabulary unlike any to which students have previously been exposed. What this student generally hears is perceived as "noise" and the student shuts down, mentally wanders off, and becomes invisible to the teacher. For example, the teacher's expectation that a student will know that a table is *not* a place at which we eat, but a chart students are supposed to consult when searching for the answer is quite naïve. It is based on the notion that the child understands the many different academic uses of the word *table* when in reality the child has not yet acquired the academic version of *table*.

In order for ELLs to become knowledgeable in the academic language of the classroom, textbooks, and curriculum, they must be taught it specifically and purposefully. This instruction additionally needs to take place in a meaningful context. Krashen distinguishes between learning and acquisition (1982, 10). The language that is initially acquired in L1 is "acquired" as opposed to "learned." He views language that is formally taught through a conscious process as less likely to be retained compared to language that is acquired in a natural setting and through meaningful use for a meaningful purpose in a meaningful context.

With Krashen's distinction in place, it is easy to see how teaching language in isolation is less productive than teaching it in a meaningful context. He posits that classrooms are often places where "learning" takes place, but should be places where "acquisition" takes place. With this in mind, it is clear that although academic language needs to be "taught," it needs to be done in a manner that leads to "acquisition."

An additional theory of Krashen is the input hypothesis. He states that all input that a student receives needs to be comprehensible (1982, 20). As stated earlier, if students do not understand the message, they will hear "noise" and the input is meaningless. Often ELLs are taught language in isolation where the English language development curriculum focuses on decontextualized vocabulary. Often ELLs are pulled out for language instruction, but while being isolated from the content classes, the ELL is losing precious time in academic instruction. As Freeman and Freeman so aptly point out, if students need to be receiving messages they understand, those messages might as well be about the standard course of study (2009, 72). By giving students comprehensible input in academic English, students are enabled to access the curriculum while simultaneously focusing on the academic language.

It is a given that academic language is key to school success and, therefore, life. However, as noted previously, many children are coming to school in both rural and urban areas speaking marginalized dialects and second languages. Therefore, it is the authors' belief that academic language is a second language for most students (O'Neal and Ringler 2010,

51). By taking this approach to language varieties and language differences, one must then take the next step, which is to evaluate how teachers deliver instruction in a way that promotes academic language literacy for both native and nonnative speakers.

There is much to be learned from all of the research that has been done in the field of teaching English as a second language, which can help improve academic language instruction.

HOW DO WE DELIVER ACADEMIC LANGUAGE INSTRUCTION?

English language learners (ELLs) are confronted with two issues: learning language and academic content simultaneously (Coleman and Goldenberg 2010, 62). In order to best address this challenge, many ESL programs have adopted content-based instructional approaches to teaching. Using a content-based approach ensures that there is focus on the content at the same time that there is focus on the academic language needed for school success. Although course content is used for this approach, the focus remains on the language development with ELLs and the assessment is on the language skills as opposed to the content.

Another model used in the ESL field has been the Sheltered Instruction Approach, which also focuses on language and course content. The big difference between these two models is that the focus of a sheltered classroom is to make the course content comprehensible to ELLs so that they will pass their grade-level standards. Obviously as part of making the content comprehensible the language will be addressed appropriately. However, in the end, it is the course content that is being assessed while CBI is assessing the language.

Although a variety of content-based models and sheltered models have been implemented over the years, the most prolific and successful is the Sheltered Instruction Observation Protocol or SIOP® model (Echevarria, Vogt, and Short 2008). It is widely used to accomplish language and content instruction through the implementation of its eight components with their thirty indicators for effective teaching. The use of the SIOP® makes the content concepts comprehensible while focusing on academic language development (Echevarria, Vogt, and Short 2008). The eight components of the SIOP® are: Lesson Preparation, Building Background, Comprehensible Input, Strategies, Interaction, Practice Application, Lesson Delivery, and Review Assessment.

When looking at other approaches that focus on academic language literacy such as the CHATS Model (Himmele and Himmele 2009) and Six Steps to Better Vocabulary Instruction (Marzano 2009), there are many overlapping concepts. Haynes and Zacarian also address numerous key characteristics to teaching ELLs across the content areas, which again mirror those expressed in CHATS and SIOP®. All of these models and strategies use visual representations, high levels of engagement, and interaction and focus on academic language development.

With the book's focus being academic language literacy for all students, both ELLs and native speakers, it is logical that a model that is designed for ELLs to blend language into content-area instruction would work. The approach in this book involves using a professional development model that will successfully work with mainstream teachers and give them the skills to focus on the language component of their content while successfully teaching to both ELLs and native speakers.

When language is taught through content, the focus can be on grammatical structures, vocabulary, and appropriate oral and written language varieties in a meaningful context. The content can then be made more comprehensible, thereby benefiting students of all language and academic backgrounds. Freeman and Freeman list four good reasons to teach academic language through content: (1) students learn both language and content, (2) the language is kept in its natural context, (3) the students find reasons to use the language for real purposes, and (4) they learn the vocabulary of their content areas (2009, 176).

AN OVERVIEW OF SIOP®, CHATS, AND SIX-STEPS

Sheltered Instruction Observation Protocol. SIOP® is a research-based model developed by Echevarria, Vogt, and Short as a means to make content concepts clear for ELLs while giving students the language skills needed for academic success (15). What has made the SIOP® so useful for the professional development activities described in this book is the variety of lesson plan formats to guide instruction, the checklist and observation protocol for teachers to observe one another, and the framework that it provided to guide meaningful instruction.

The beauty of the SIOP® model has been its ability to act as the framework for all other initiatives that a school has in place. For example, the authors are often greeted with apprehension about taking on a new project and having the teachers perceive this as the next fad to come along. This reaction is understandable given the number of times teachers are subjected to the "latest and greatest" only to see it disappear the next year. This model, however, has connected on many levels to existing initiatives but has language as its keystone. Teachers begin to see how the SIOP® allows them to interject language into their cooperative learning experiences, how it requires academic language responses both orally and in writing, and how it incorporates graphic organizers like Thinking Maps® (Hyerle 2004).

One frequent comment from teachers is that these models are all just "good teaching" and the authors have to concur that it is so, except for one major difference: the strong emphasis on academic language development. Himmele and Himmele add to the discussion by stating that good teaching also pays attention to language through scaffolding that is "informed by an understanding of students' language development" (2009, 5).

An overview of the SIOP® can be only that: an overview. Full understanding of the model and the skill set needed to implement it with fidelity can only be obtained by going through intensive training. The publishers of the model provide this training and those who have been trained via the trainer model, as the authors have. With that in mind, the authors will share the

Table 2.3. Eight Components of the SIOP®

Lesson Preparation	Language and content objectives written in student-friendly language and read by the students
Building Background	Links made to students' background, past learning, and academic vocabulary
Comprehensible Input	Content delivered through whatever means needed to make clear, often visually and through use of realia
Strategies	Learning strategies emphasized—often with the use of graphic organizers and higher-order questioning
Interaction	Language is a social interaction and must be used with others to provide ample opportunities for practice with academic language
Practice and Application	Use of hands-on meaningful activities to process the content in a meaningful way
Lesson Delivery	Serves as a checklist for the teacher to reflect on whether the objectives were met and whether the lesson was appropriately paced
Review and Assessment	Reiterates that assessment must be adapted to the language needs of the students and that assessment is both formative and summative

eight components (see table 2.3) of the SIOP®, and then show the common threads that weave through the CHATS model and Marzano's Six Steps.

While the SIOP® requires that all eight components be present for an effective sheltered lesson to take place, it is understood that not all lessons will have all eight components each day. In other words, as teachers plan their unit, they need to be certain that from beginning to end, all eight pieces are evident.

The CHATS Model. Like the SIOP®, CHATS is viewed not as a scripted approach, but as a framework for simultaneous content and language development. The authors of the model state that its best use is by teachers co-teaching; however, they state that it can be effectively used in all types of teaching situations with all types of learners (Himmele and Himmele 2009). This is especially compelling to us as the authors started using the SIOP® solely for improving instruction for ELLs until teachers all professed how well it helped all of their students. Thanks to a trusting professional relationship with the authors, teachers and administrators successfully applied a model proven to work with ELLs with a different group of students, SELs. The successful implementation of this model was attributed to ongoing job-embedded professional development that incorporated analysis and reflection of the impact of academic language literacy strategies on student learning.

The basis of the CHATS model is that content is learned through language and language must have some content in order to be acquired. The relationship between the two is undeniable, yet in the past language often was taught in isolated vacuums using vocabulary unrelated to the class work or to any relevant content. This interrelationship supports the use of content-based and sheltered instructional models. Using the CHATS model as a framework encourages teachers to be attentive to the language needs of the students. Table 2.4 below provides an overview of the five components of CHATS.

Content reading strategies refer to the teacher helping students comprehend the components of academic text and helping them find ways to best navigate the new vocabulary. Teachers explain how to decipher words in context, how to understand the structure of academic text, and how to make sense of the text (Himmele and Himmele 2009). The student component consists of giving students strategies to organize and make sense of the new content and academic vocabulary through the use of a variety of graphic organizers.

Higher-order thinking skills are based on using Bloom's Taxonomy to guide questioning to a deeper level. Himmele and Himmele refer us to Vygotsky, who views academic language and higher-order questioning as a

Table 2.4. The CHATS Model

C=Content Reading Strategies	Teacher guided comprehension strategies Meta-cognitive strategies for students to include graphic organizers
H=Higher Order Thinking Questions	Moving from the lower level of the Bloom's Taxonomy to the higher-order questions
A=Assessment	Empower the teacher with assessment strategies to monitor progress
T=Total Participation Techniques	Increasing the level of active engagement for the ALL students
S=Scaffolding Strategies	Planning for the bridging activities that bring students from what they can do to where you want them to be

reciprocal relationship. In other words, they encourage the development of each other and act in a cyclical way: the more higher-order questions asked, the more academic language used and the more the academic language develops, the more higher-order questioning can take place. If students are kept at the lower level of knowledge-based questioning, then the approach reverts to merely supporting memorization of lists.

Assessment is based on the premise that classroom teachers are often not part of the language assessment process and do not have a clear understanding of language development. This section of CHATS provides the teacher with a variety of techniques to provide ongoing assessment in the classroom. Additionally, it informs the educator about the stages of language acquisition in second-language learners. For the purposes of this book, all learners are second-language learners since academic language is not native to or the L1 of any of the students.

Total participation techniques encourage the teacher to implement strategies that highly engage all students. If language is viewed from a social interactionist's perspective, one realizes the value of classroom strategies that value interaction and cooperative learning styles. Working in small groups first and then building to larger groups and finally to whole groups provides multiple opportunities for students to practice using their academic language in a safe setting. Again, in order for students to become successful with school and academic language acquisition, they must have ample opportunities to listen, speak, read, and write the target language: academic language.

Scaffolding approaches teaching from the perspective that one cannot expect students to go from where they currently are to where one wants them to advance without instructional support strategies. This is very reminiscent of Vygotsky's zone of proximal development, which emphasizes the role the teacher has as a guide. The image that scaffolding evokes of a laddered or tiered approach to teaching and learning is helpful to remind teachers that we must go one step at a time to achieve our instructional goals.

Marzano's Six Steps to Better Vocabulary Instruction. According to Marzano, students require academic language fluency in order to be successful academically. He makes a direct connection to poverty by stating that impoverished children are exposed to much less language than children from working-class and professional families (2004, 10). The fact is that all students, whether they are native English speakers or ELLs, need proficiency in academic language. Marzano's approach to building background is to look at the lack of experiences children of poverty have and the resulting lack of exposure to academic language (2004, 12). He looks at vocabulary building as a six-step approach (see table 2.5). Like the SIOP® and CHATS, his research shows that all six components need to be evident for successful vocabulary acquisition that results in the new language becoming fully integrated with the student's active working vocabulary.

Marzano comments that teachers often try many strategies, some good and some bad, but more often than not it is *how* the strategy is implemented that determines its success (2009, 84). A recurring theme with all of these approaches and strategies is that like baking a cake, if one ingredient is left out, it is not the same cake. The six-step approach needs to include all six steps to ensure the success of the strategy and the retention of the new vocabulary.

A key point that stands out with this approach is the recognition that all too often teachers write definitions on a board, have students copy and memorize the definition, and then expect the student to understand the

Table 2.5. Marzano's Six-Step Approach to Better Vocabulary

Explain new term	Teacher explains new term in a comprehensible manner
Student restates new term	Student restates in own words, showing comprehension of new term
Visually represent new term	Students draw or construct a visual representation of new term
Engage in activities with new term	Students are provided multiple engaging activities in which to use new term
Discuss new term with others	Students orally discuss new term with classmates
Use games that reinforce new term	Games are used as a means to reinforce new term

word. Marzano points out that it is the student's ability to restate the meaning in his or her own words that helps develop an awareness of the new vocabulary (2009, 84). By so doing, the new definition written in the student's notebook is far more meaningful than the one copied directly from the board.

Marzano's research also shows that creating a visual connection to the new word is essential to making an imprint of sorts for the student. This also provides an opportunity for the teacher to formatively assess whether the student has complete comprehension of the new term. Additionally, it gives the child a chance to explain the picture to the class and use the vocabulary in a meaningful way to reinforce its place in their personal knowledge bank.

CONNECTING THE DOTS: HOW DO THESE THREE MODELS OVERLAP?

It is quite evident from looking at the SIOP®, CHATS, and Six-Steps that there are common themes among them. How do they connect and where? Table 2.6 is a visual representation of the three models aligned with key components of effective language instruction.

As table 2.6 shows, these models all overlap, which is essential in understanding the authors' choice of the SIOP® for the context of these professional development activities. It enabled the authors to have an umbrella under which they were able to shelter all of the other initiatives that were already in place in the schools. For example, many schools had already received Thinking Maps® training and were concerned about having to incorporate a new model. After deep and thorough discussions, it became evident that this approach was giving them a context in which to apply their graphic visual language. This new context was the development and encouragement of academic language proficiency across all content areas. This approach is helping make content teachers aware of their responsibility to teach the academic language in a meaningful way that will yield both academic and linguistic achievement.

SUMMARY

Children come to school speaking social language and learn academic language in school. Because people do not speak in formal academic language at home, it follows that students are acquiring a second language for school

Table 2.6. SIOP® CHATS, and Six-Steps Key Components of Effective Language Instruction

Components of Effective Language Instruction	SIOP®	CHATS	Six-Steps
Background Knowledge	Entire component devoted to building background.	Scaffolding serves to bridge students and make connections.	Students explain new term using examples from their experiences.
Engagement and Interaction	Entire component based on the effectiveness of interactive activities.	Total participation techniques engage students in using academic language.	Students engage in activities to use new term, play games with new vocabulary.
Visual Representations	Comprehensible input, strategies, practice application, and assessment all target visually representing content vocabulary.	Content reading strategies incorporate the use of graphic organizers for visual representations.	Students visually represent the new term.
Higher-Order Questioning & Thinking	Strategies component has HOTS at its core.	H=Higher-order questioning as a key part of the model.	No clear direction for use of HOTS.
Scaffolding	Strategies component clearly presents scaffolding as a key part of the section.	S=Scaffolding strategies.	Students restate the new term in their words, which serves as a means of scaffolding.
Assessment	Assessment is a key component of the model. It serves as a formative tool.	A=Assessment.	Visual representation of the new term serves as a formative assessment strategy.

success—the language of the test, texts, and content. Krashen's Monitor Hypothesis talks about *learning* a language versus *acquiring* a language where the goal is to *acquire* the language while engaging in meaningful content learning activities (Krashen 1982, 10). According to Krashen, when a student *learns a language* the teacher uses strategies that are specific to teaching a language, such as memorization of content, skill and drill, and repetition drills (ex. choral response or writing words over and over). This language instruction is often divided in chunks and not typically connected to the context of the content.

Many adults can remember taking a French or Spanish class and repeating scripted conversations and memorizing verb tenses. Many adults will often say that they do not remember much of the language that was learned. Take this analogy into classrooms. Many students will say they do not remember much of what they learned after they took the test because they were studying for the test. Classrooms that adopt Krashen's acquisition model are places where students learn academic language, as they understand the content.

It is important to understand that even though content teachers are not language teachers, they can use language acquisition strategies to teach their content. Several frameworks were discussed in this chapter: SIOP®, CHATS, and Marzano's vocabulary strategies. These frameworks are effective and doable for teachers. The authors of these models have published books that are conducive to professional learning communities of teachers to read and implement. It is important to remember that teachers need time to learn language strategies and use these strategies in the classroom, and opportunities to see the results for themselves. The principal's role is to facilitate time and opportunities to implement and provide feedback. Feedback and reflection are key skills in working through implementation obstacles. Chapter 5 outlines strategies for effective implementation of professional development that focuses on academic language proficiency.

WORKS CITED

Bielenberg, Brian, and Lily Wong Fillmore. "The English They Need for the Test." *Educational Leadership* 62.4 (2004): 45–49.

Chamot, Anna Uhl, and J. Michael O'Malley. *The CALLA Handbook: Implementing the Cognitive Academic Language Learning Approach.* Boston: Addison-Wesley, 1994.

Coleman, Rhoda, and Claude Goldenberg. "What Does Research Say about Effective Practices for English Learners? Part II: Academic Language Proficiency." *Kappa Delta Pi Record* 46.2 (2010): 60–65.

Corson, David. "The Learning and Use of Academic English Words." *Language Learning* 47.4 (1997): 671–718.

Coxhead, Averil. "A New Academic Word List." *TESOL Quarterly* 34.2 (2000): 213–38.

Cummins, Jim. *Bilingualism and Special Education: Program and Pedagogical Issues.* Clevedon: Multilingual Matters, 1984.

———. *Language, Power and Pedagogy: Bilingual Children in the Crossfire.* Tonawanda: Multilingual Matters, 2000.

Echevarria, Jana, MaryEllen Vogt, and Deborah Short. *Making Content Comprehensible for English Language Learners: The SIOP Model*. 3rd Edition. Boston: Pearson Education, 2008.

Freeman, Yvonne, and David Freeman. *Academic Language for English Language Learners and Struggling Readers: How to Help Students Succeed Across the Content Areas*. Portsmouth: Heinemann, 2009.

Goldenberg, Claude, and Rhoda Coleman. *Promoting Academic Achievement Among English Learners*. Thousand Oaks: Corwin, 2010.

Haynes, Judie, and Debbie Zacarian. *Teaching English Language Learners: Across the Content Areas*. Alexandria: Association for Supervision & Curriculum Development, 2010.

Himmele, Persida, and William Himmele. *The Language Rich Classroom: A Research Based Framework for Teaching English Language Learners*. 2nd Edition. Alexandria: Association for Supervision and Curriculum Development, 2009.

Hyerle, David N. *Student Success with Thinking Maps: School-based Research, Results, and Models for Achievement Using Visual Tools*. Thousand Oaks: Corwin, 2004.

Krashen, Stephen. *Principles and Practices of Second Language Acquisition*. Oxford: Pergamon, 1982.

Marzano, Robert. *Building Background Knowledge for Academic Achievement: Research on What Works in Schools*. Alexandria: Association of Supervision and Curriculum Development, 2004.

———. "Six Steps to Better Vocabulary Instruction." *Educational Leadership* 67.1 (2009): 83–84.

Nieto, Sonia. "Chapter 3: We Speak Many Tongues: Language Diversity and Multicultural Education." In *Language, Culture and Teaching: Critical Perspectives for a New Century*, 79–100. Mahwah: Lawrence Erlbaum, 2002.

O'Neal, Debra, and Marjorie Ringler. "Broadening our View of Linguistic Diversity." *Phi Delta Kappan* 91.7 (2010): 48–52.

Vygotsky, Lev. *Thought and Language*. Cambridge: MIT Press, 1986.

Wolfram, Walt, and Natalie Shilling-Estes. *American English: Dialects and Variations*. 2nd Edition. Malden: Blackwell, 2006.

❸

CONTENT

Specific Strategies for Academic Language Literacy

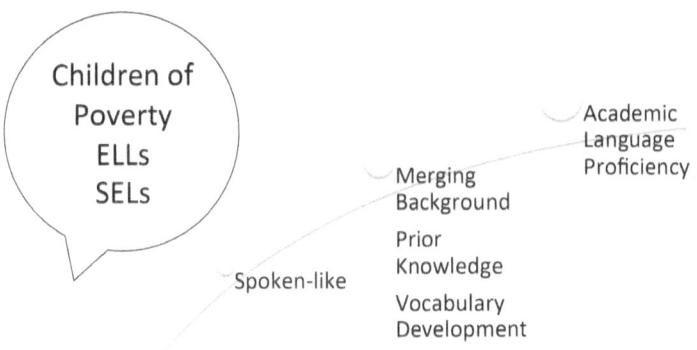

Chapter 3 Organizer

The chapter organizer graphic provides a visual of the elements that help reach academic language proficiency. It is important to understand students' linguistic diversity for the selection of teaching and learning strategies. Understanding students' spoken language is an essential task in understanding children of poverty, standard English learners (SELs), and English language learners (ELLs). These students' language skills are mostly oral and dialectal, and lack vocabulary and background knowledge needed to learn content in schools.

To reach academic language proficiency, teachers need to merge learning with each child's background experiences, build background knowledge, access prior knowledge, and build vocabulary. The more teachers take the time to focus on vocabulary development, building background knowledge, and connecting to students' experiences, the more students will be able to transition from spoken-like language to academic language.

This chapter describes and provides examples of two types of strategies, instructional and learning, that help students learn academic language. Typically, instructional strategies that focus on language are taught to students who are ELLs. However, ELLs are not the only linguistically diverse students. SELs' linguistic diversity was described in chapter 2. Linguistically speaking, everyone is different and so are students. Each individual has a dialect and varying background experiences that influence learning. Therefore it is important for teachers to understand *who* they are *really* teaching.

Teachers are teaching students who possess a language difference (Spanish, French, Hmong, etc.); students who speak a dialect other than standard English; and students who lack required background knowledge (vocabulary deficient). Once teachers understand *who* they are really teaching then they will realize that *what* they are *really* teaching is academic language!

Here are three reasons why it is important to use academic language strategies (a more in-depth description of academic language instruction can be found in chapter 2):

- Academic success requires academic language literacy (O'Neal and Ringler 2010, 51)
- Students who lack background knowledge often lack academic language proficiency (Marzano 2004)
- Children who speak marginalized dialects are not proficient in academic language (Nieto 2002)

The purpose of this book is to show how academic language is the equalizer for all learners. All learners need academic language—regardless of their native language, dialect, or background knowledge. This is why all content area teachers need to teach the language component of their content. Teachers need to see themselves not just as science, math, or social studies teachers; they are language teachers. There are many models/frameworks explained in chapter 2 that help teach the content and language of a subject. This chapter provides strategies for linguistically diverse students whose target language is academic language. Teachers need to learn language-teaching strategies in order to teach students a new language: academic language.

STRATEGIES FOR A LINGUISTICALLY DIVERSE CLASSROOM

The beginning of this chapter established that content teachers do not see themselves as language teachers, even though they are. This section provides instructional and learning strategies to use when teaching the language of content. Keeping in mind that students come to school to learn academic language, it follows that students are second-language learners. Research shows that second-language learners use strategies, *but good* language learners use more varied strategies.

Strategy instruction improves academic performance. Strategies must be taught so that students can use them. Students do not know language acquisition strategies and therefore teachers must take the time to teach the strategies. Strategies make mentally active learners and thus are effective in learning academic language (O'Malley and Chamot 1990). Teachers will know when students have internalized learning strategies when students transfer these strategies to new tasks. It is important to understand what is meant by instructional strategies and by learning strategies.

Instructional strategies are activities, techniques, approaches, and methods that *teachers* use to promote student learning and achievement (techniques).

Learning strategies are conscious, flexible plans *learners* use to make sense of what they're reading and learning (learner-centered).

Strategies may be both instructional and learning. It depends on who is using the strategies and for what purpose. The next section describes several strategies that teachers may use as instructional strategies. With continual use, the goal is for students to use them independently as learning strategies.

ACADEMIC LANGUAGE LEARNING STRATEGIES

Academic language learning strategies encourage students to listen, speak, read, and write in academic language. This section describes vocabulary-building strategies, academic writing strategies, and higher-order thinking strategies that incorporate one or more opportunities to listen, speak, read, and write in academic language. There are many more academic language strategies; the hope is that the strategies included in this chapter will spark conversation among teachers about the use of strategies to improve academic language literacy and academic language proficiency.

A common misconception about teaching academic language is that teachers *only* teach content vocabulary. Even though learning content vocabulary is essential for academic success, it is important to use academic language strategies to make connections across content and compare the vocabulary to social context or academic processes of higher-order thinking. The next section describes some vocabulary-building strategies and the following sections continue with reading and writing strategies.

Vocabulary Building

Adequate comprehension depends on knowing 90–95 percent of words in a text (Hirsch 2003, 16). Think about special education students, hearing impaired students, children of poverty, and English learners. These groups of students, to name a few, start out with a smaller vocabulary. Teaching vocabulary is necessary because it improves comprehension for ALL learners (McKeown, Beck, and Omanson 1985, 522). Here are some of the authors' favorite strategies that teachers have used with positive results.

Four-square. A four-square is a simple graphic organizer that helps students learn and retain their knowledge of vocabulary. The strategy is to divide a paper in four squares:

- First quadrant: The student writes the vocabulary word.
- Second quadrant: The student draws a picture to represent the definition of a word.
- Third quadrant: The student writes a synonym of the word.
- Fourth quadrant: The student writes a sentence (using context clues) correctly using the word.

Four-Squares and Academic Language Proficiency. In the authors' work with academic language proficiency, teachers are encouraged to use four-squares by placing students in collaborative groups. Group work naturally has students speak about the assignment, listen to each other's use of academic language, and write and read the information on the four-squares in academic language. At the end of the four-square activity each group shares their product. Some common ways of sharing include presentations or gallery walks, which also reinforce listening, speaking, reading, and writing academic language.

Figurative language is an essential part of academic language (Zwiers 2008). Examples of figurative language in academic language include expressions such as: *boils down to, sidestep an issue, read between the lines, outweigh, the answer does not hold water, the elephant in the room, set the stage for.* Students don't typically speak with such academic expressions as these; therefore, when teachers use these expressions they may not be aware that they may be confusing a student who has not developed academic language proficiency. This book is not saying to stop using these expressions; on the contrary, these expressions are present in academic language. Teachers need to be aware of the use of the expressions and teach them to students in order to keep using the expressions.

Figurative language also includes idioms. Idioms are higher-order language strategies that must be taught. For students who are not academic language proficient or are English learners, idioms are barriers to learning academic language. Students may learn idioms using four-squares. Figure 3.1 provides an example meant for students to work in groups to complete the four-square:

- First quadrant: The students write the idiom.
- Second quadrant: The students draw a picture of the literal meaning of the idiom. Drawing a picture of the literal meaning helps the teacher understand what students picture in their heads when they see an idiom that they do not understand. The picture of the literal meaning helps students remember in a fun way what the idiom does *not* mean. Also, for students who are not academic language proficient, drawing may be a significant contribution to the group activity. All students have something to contribute—even if they do not speak the language!

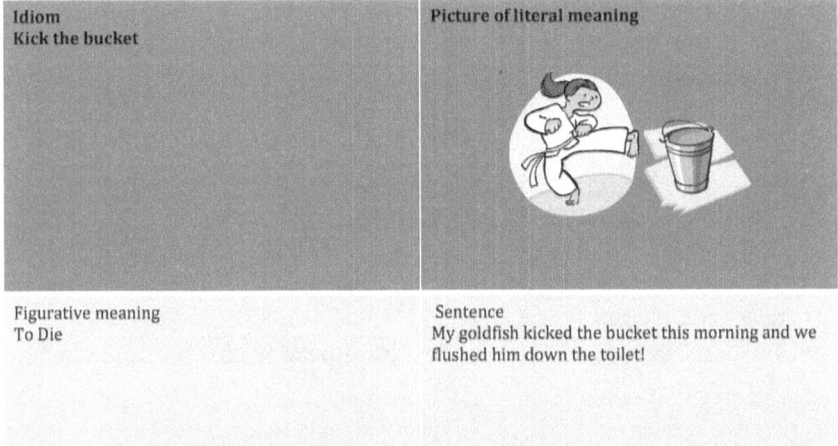

Figure 3.1. Example of an Idiom Four-Square

- Third quadrant: The students write the figurative meaning. Working in groups, students speak, listen, read, and write about the idiom. Students help each other understand a difficult language concept.
- Fourth quadrant: The students write an academic sentence using the idiom and context clues.

Personal Dictionaries. All students keeps their own personal dictionary of words that are challenging to them. Four-squares may be used as the template for a personal dictionary. It is impossible to do a four-square for each and every word on a vocabulary list. The authors recommend that students self-select words that they have difficulty with and use this strategy. On this same note, research discourages the use of vocabulary lists and activities that do not provide a meaningful context to learn words. Vocabulary work such as defining a list of words is more a memorization strategy than a learning strategy. Remember that students need to listen, speak, read, and write in academic language to become proficient; therefore, selecting a strategy that can include all or most of the modes of language is essential.

Modified Word Walls. Word walls are commonly used in elementary schools and provide a place on a wall where the vocabulary words for the lesson are displayed. The words are typically written on sentence strips and teachers often pull the words and use them during instruction. In this scenario, students are able to listen and read the vocabulary words.

A modified version of a word wall (Wagstaff 1999) is applicable to K–12 grade levels. The modified version provides an organizer that helps students link to prior knowledge and learn vocabulary in meaningful contexts. Figure 3.2 illustrates an example of a modified word wall. The strategy is to complete this modified version of the word wall throughout the instruction of a lesson:

- First list the new words to be learned in the lesson in the first box.
- The next box lists the words in the lesson that students know in a different context but have a new meaning in this lesson.
- The next box lists the people associated with the content of the lesson.
- The next box lists words in the lesson that are "everyday" words but are necessary for this lesson.
- The last box lists words to review from previous lessons that apply to this lesson.

This modified word wall is an effective teaching strategy to help students connect old learning to new learning. This word wall can also be used as

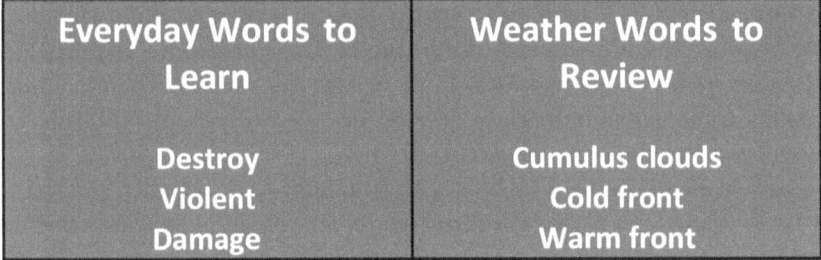

Figure 3.2. Modified Word Wall

a framework for assessment of student learning. In order to improve academic language proficiency, students should write in academic language. One extension activity could be to have students write several paragraphs about what they learned in this lesson by using the word wall as a framework for their writing.

Shades of Meaning (Goodman 2004, 85). The shades of meaning strategy helps expand vocabulary by encouraging students to brainstorm words to describe different variations of the same concept. The strategy is to

- Bring in paint chip cards from a hardware store;
- Explain the meaning of *shades* (degrees);
- Also explain other meanings of the word *shade* (sunglasses, under a tree, curtains); and
- Generate a word list for a particular word and then rank them by shades of meaning

Each time the authors had teachers use this strategy; they got excited about the activity. By using shades of meaning, teachers saw how the strategy promotes the use of academic language by asking students to justify (using academic language) the rationale for suggesting a ranking for a word. For example, in training a group of teachers the word "collaboration" was placed in the middle. Teachers were asked to find words that described higher degrees of collaboration and lower degrees of collaboration and explain their rationale for the rank. The discussions that ensued were higher order and with a high use of academic language. Teachers listed professional learning communities as higher ranking after having a discussion about the different types of learning communities that fall in two categories (healthy and unhealthy). Teachers also listed isolation in the lowest degree as the ultimate example of non-collaboration. Teachers listed many words in between and learned many concepts about collaboration in this activity.

Students do well with this activity. Some teachers scaffold this activity by providing the words to use in the rankings and some teachers have students use the dictionary to help them with this activity. There are many modifications possible that can only be made after trying the activity and understanding the benefits and challenges.

Rest in Peace (RIP). Teachers with students create a bulletin board for RIP words by identifying overused words and create new words that can replace them. The Shades of Meaning activity on age 41 provides a great way to find new words to replace overused words.

- Ex: nice
- I met a nice girl today.
- Replace with: I met a very friendly girl today.

Using Morphology. Teaching morphology helps students construct meanings of words that they may not know by using roots. A word generation strategy is helpful for learning roots.

- Have students discuss the meaning of a root. Examples of roots: scrib or script, rupt, miss or mit, tact.
- Have students list all the words they know that have a certain root.
- Have students discuss the different words and how the root is important to the definition of the word.

This activity is fun for students. When students are challenged (in groups) to list as many words as possible that contain a root, they often get competitive and use the dictionary to find more words. While completing the challenge, each student in a group is listening, speaking, reading, and writing vocabulary based on morphology.

Often when the authors train, the word "port" is used to demonstrate this strategy. The root "port" means "to carry." Lists typically include words such as import, export, report, and support. Many times the word "sport" is added to the list. This is an excellent opportunity to discuss the meaning of "port" and to decide as a group whether "sport" belongs on the list. The discussions and rationales often strike "sport" from the list because in this case "port" is not used as a root by adding an "s" as the prefix; however, the learning that occurred in this discussion is higher order.

Similarly, the word "Portobello" as in "Portobello mushroom" is discussed and each group that has the discussion provides a rationale for or against. The authors let the groups decide whether the word belongs or not depending on the academic argument they provide. Many say that the word "bello" means beautiful and that "Portobello" is an adjective describing "carrying beauty." Some don't see the connection. The value is in the discussion of the root and the fact that students will often remember the definition of "port" thanks to the strategy used.

Reading and Writing Strategies

Written academic language has its conceptions (see chapter 2) and these must be taught. Students need to understand how academic language is different from social language in both written and spoken forms. Often teachers assume that students are able to develop their own strategies to write in academic language. This is a common mistake that can be easily addressed by focusing on academic language instruction while teaching content. Strategies in this section help students read and write academic language.

Sentence Frames. Sentence frames provide opportunities for students to practice writing and speaking in multiple contexts by giving students a framework for academic structures that are unfamiliar. Sentence frames create academic language habits for speaking and writing. The authors always include this strategy in professional development because it can be used across the curriculum.

Sentence frames provide a framework for explicitly expecting students to use academic language and help students write summaries, take notes, shape written products, and make oral presentations. As the students internalize academic structures for speaking and writing academic language, the sentence frames become less of a strategy and more of the way students communicate about the content. Some examples of sentence frames follow.

- Communities consist of _____.
- In conclusion, all _____.

- I expected _____ to happen; however, the lab proved that _____.
- After reading the book, the key message I learned was _____.
- When dividing fractions you must _____.
- I think _____ is going to happen because _____.
- At first I thought _____, but now I think _____.

Paragraph Frame. Paragraph frames are similar to sentence frames. Many argue that providing paragraph frames limits the student's ability to write creatively. This book is not saying that paragraph frames should be used at all times. What the book is saying is that students do not instinctively write in academic language structures. Typically students "write as they speak." The spoken language of students is not academic in nature. Therefore, if students are expected to write in academic language, they need to learn how to structure their writing academically. Paragraph frames provide a strategy for students to follow as they learn to write in academic language. The teacher and students are expected to use other creative academic writing strategies as they become proficient in written academic language (Celic 2009, 183).

HOTS Strategy. Students are taught how to write responses to higher-order-thinking skills (HOTS) questions. In order to do so, teachers must plan the higher-order questions ahead of time. Planning the questions ahead of time ensures that higher-order thinking is central to the lesson. Teachers need to spend some time teaching students about the higher-order-thinking skills and helping students identify the different types of higher-order-thinking skills along with the ways to respond according to the skill. Therefore, when a teacher poses a higher-order-thinking question, the student should first identify the higher-order-thinking skill that applies to the question and then use the strategies to respond orally or in writing to the question.

In education, Marzano's and Bloom's levels of questioning (Anderson and Krathwohl 2001) are widely accepted and expected to be used in classrooms (Marzano 1993, 155). Even though these researchers' frameworks for higher-order thinking are available, teachers continue to use lower-order thinking as common practice. Published research (Tienken, Goldberg, and Dirocco 2009, 41) confirmed research from the 1980s that indicated that 60–80 percent of teacher questions were at literal or knowledge level. In the authors' visits to schools and work with teachers, they also noticed that the majority of questions posed by teachers were at the literal level.

Bricks and Mortar. The bricks and mortar (Zwiers 2008) activity provides the opportunity for students to manipulate language in order to develop academic sentences. In this strategy, bricks are the key content vocabulary and mortar are the academic words that tie the concepts together (cause/effect, verbs, transition words, conjunctions).

- Give students an envelope with different-colored cards or pieces of paper: one color for bricks and one color for mortar.
- Students discuss words and write a sentence using their cards.

Expect sentences to be written in academic language. This is a nonnegotiable expectation. Students' products should be in academic language. The more they use academic language, the more fluent they will be.

Hierarchical Graphic Organizers (Celic 2009, 148). This strategy provides the opportunity for students to manipulate language in order to develop academic sentences.

- Give students cards with the essential information of the lesson.
- Give students a blank tree map with the appropriate spaces.
- After students place all of the cards, they write sentences. Expect sentences to be written in academic language. Be explicit of the expectation of complete sentences and inclusion of certain key concepts, language, and/or sentence structures.

Split Page Note-Taking (Vogt and Echevarria 2007, 88)

- Create a T-chart/fold paper in half.
- Left side: students preview reading and write questions predicting what they believe the text will answer using WH (who, what, when, where, why)—questions.
- Students read text in groups.
- Students answer questions in groups. Expect answers to be written in academic language. Be explicit of the expectation of the use of complete sentences and inclusion of certain key concepts, language, and/or sentence structures.

Graphic Organizers for Note-Taking or Deciphering Text. Graphic organizers help students visualize and organize content. Figure 3.3 provides an example that may be used when viewing video or reading dense texts. In this graphic organizer, students may list the participants in the excerpt or

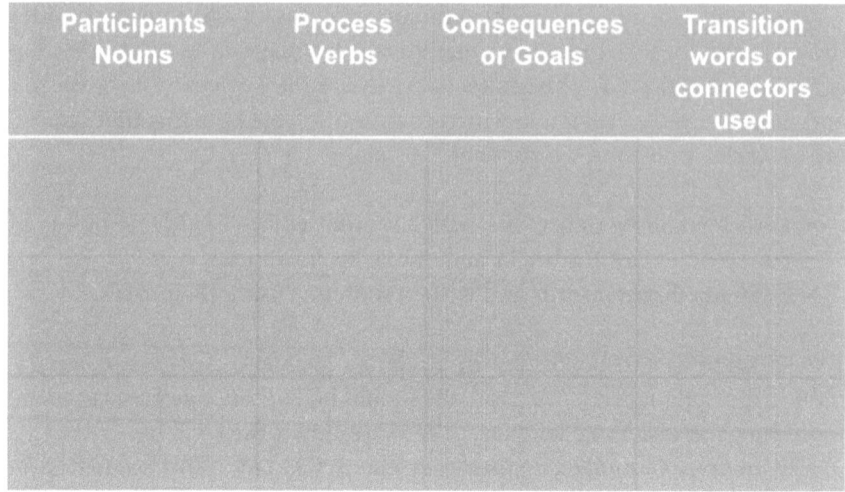

Figure 3.3. Graphic Organizer for Deciphering Text

video, noting that each participant constitutes a noun in written text. The action, process, or event is typically a verb. Each action, process, or event has a consequence or attains a goal typically listed after a transition word.

This strategy uses language strategies to decipher text. Students may look for nouns, verbs, and transition words to get clues and determine key people, what happened (verbs), what the results were. In the same manner, students may use their notes to write a complete sentence or paragraph that describes who, what, why by using language structures that include nouns, verbs, and transition words.

Graphic Organizer for Concept Definition. Understanding of a concept is key for student learning. Often in teacher-centered classrooms teachers tell the students the concepts and assume that students understood the concepts. This graphic organizer for concept definition provides an opportunity for students to produce their understanding of a concept. The authors strongly encourage that this organizer be completed in groups because students will have the opportunity to listen, speak, read, and write the academic language associated with a concept.

For this strategy, students in a group discuss and reach consensus on the definition of a concept. They are asked to provide examples of the concepts and list any related terms or issues about the concept. In many of the authors' professional developments, teachers define linguistic diversity and list examples and related terms. Once the group is finished, they are asked to orally present their definition.

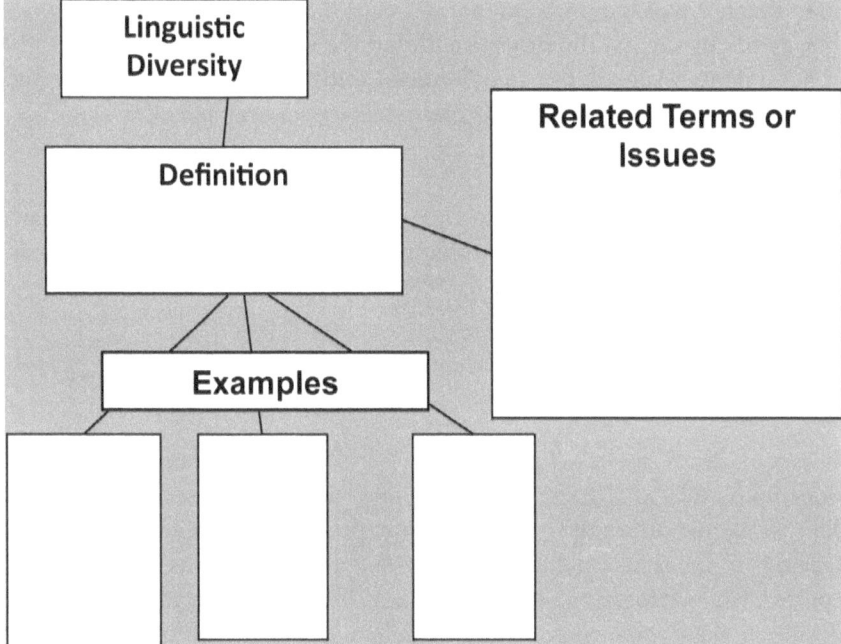

Figure 3.4. Concept Definition Graphic Organizer

Comparing all of the concept definitions and reaching consensus on one definition can expand this strategy. This definition becomes the definition for the class and is used in instruction. The fact that all in the class developed the definition creates ownership and engages students in learning even more because they created key knowledge that is now being built upon. Figure 3.4 provides a template for concept organizer strategy.

Error Correction Manual. Interactive journals provide opportunities for students to write in academic language. As the rigor of curriculum increases, academic writing becomes a measure of academic proficiency. The error correction manual is a clever tool for students to analyze a content problem, describe an error, and write a solution to an error.

Many teachers do not consider writing an essential part of their curriculum. In the authors' interactions with mathematics, physical education, and fine arts teachers (to name a few contents), teachers often share that they do not see how their subject lends itself to writing academic language. This strategy provides a great opportunity to write for all content areas—even those that do not seem likely to provide these opportunities.

- Teacher writes a problem on the board that is solved incorrectly.
- Students discuss the process and find the error.
- Students write a letter to a fictitious student describing the error and providing a correction to the error. Here is an example of an error correction manual that uses a paragraph frame:

Enrique, you got this problem wrong. You used _____, but should have used _____. When you did this problem you forgot to _____. If you remember to _____ you will _____.

SUMMARY

In chapter 2 we discussed Krashen's research on second-language acquisition and its relevance to learning academic language as a second language. The strategies presented in this chapter provide ways and examples for teachers to focus on teaching academic language. The focus is on teaching content while infusing academic language learning strategies. Acquisition occurs in classrooms where students meaningfully engage in communicative activities.

Communicative activities engage students to work in groups while listening, speaking, reading, and writing academic language. The higher-order-thinking work they complete can and should be fun. Learning is a social event and the more engaged the students are the more fun it can be!

Academic language learning strategies should always *expect* students to use academic language when they speak. It is important to remember that academic language needs to be taught and therefore teachers should scaffold for academic language use. An effective strategy for teachers is to write language objectives that identify language structures needed for lessons. Language objectives should develop academic and content-specific vocabulary, in addition to academic language process words, and higher-order-thinking processes (Echevarria, Vogt, and Short 2008, 25). Figure 3.5 provides a four-square framework to help plan for language objectives.

Above all, teachers need to model use of academic language at all times. Being aware of one's own dialects is important so that one can code-switch and use academic language during academic learning. Students model their teachers and therefore teachers need to model the use of academic language.

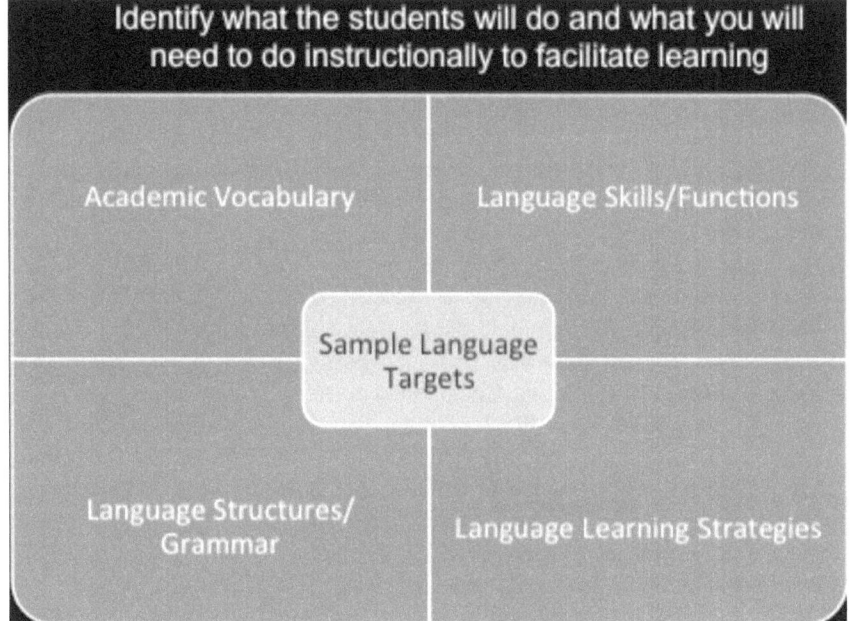

Figure 3.5. Strategy for Writing Language Objectives

WORKS CITED

Anderson, L. W., and D. L. Krathwohl. *A Taxonomy for Learning, Teaching, and Assessing: A Revision of Bloom's Taxonomy of Educational Objectives*. New York: Longman, 2001.

Celic, Christina M. *English Language Learners Day by Day, K–6*. Portsmouth: Heinemann, 2009.

Echevarria, Jana, MaryEllen Vogt, and Deborah Short. *Making Content Comprehensible for English Language Learners: The SIOP Model*. 3rd Edition. Boston: Pearson Education, 2008.

Goodman, Laurie. "Shades of Meaning: Relating and Expanding Word Knowledge." In *Teaching Vocabulary: 50 Creative Strategies, Grades K–12*, edited by G. E. Tompkins and C. Blanchfield, 85–87. Upper Saddle River: Merrill Prentice Hall, 2004.

Hirsch, E. D. Jr. "Reading Comprehension Requires Knowledge of Words and the World: Scientific Insights into the Fourth-Grade Slump and the Nation's Stagnant Comprehension Scores." *American Educator* (2003): 10–29.

Krashen, Stephen. *Principles and Practices of Second Language Acquisition*. Oxford: Pergamon, 1982.

Marzano, Robert. "How Classroom Teachers Approach the Teaching of Thinking." *Theory into Practice* 32.3 (1993): 154–60.

———. *Building Background Knowledge for Academic Achievement: Research on What Works in Schools*. Alexandria: Association of Supervision and Curriculum Development, 2004.

McKeown, Margaret, et al. "Some Effects of the Nature and Frequency of Vocabulary Instruction on the Knowledge and Use of Words." *Reading Research Quarterly* 20.5 (1985): 522–35.

Nieto, Sonia. "Chapter 3: We Speak Many Tongues: Language Diversity and Multicultural Education." In *Language, Culture and Teaching: Critical Perspectives for a New Century*, 79–100. Mahwah: Lawrence Erlbaum, 2002.

O'Malley, Michael, and Anna Uhl Chamot. *Learning Strategies in Second Language Acquisition*. Cambridge: Cambridge University Press, 1990.

O'Neal, Debra, and Marjorie Ringler. "Broadening our View of Linguistic Diversity." *Phi Delta Kappan* 91.7 (2010): 48–52.

Tienken, Christopher H., Stephanie Goldberg, and Dominic Dirocco. "Questioning the Questions." *Kappa Delta Pi Record* 46.1 (2009): 39–43.

Vogt, MaryEllen, and Jana Echevarria. *99 Ideas and Activities for Teaching English Learners with the SIOP Model*. Boston: Pearson, 2007.

Wagstaff, Janiel. *Teaching Reading and Writing with Word Walls*. New York: Scholastic, 1999.

Zwiers, Jeff. *Building Academic Language: Essential Practices for Content Classrooms*. Hoboken: Wiley, 2008.

CONTEXT

Creating Chief Education Officers (CEOs)

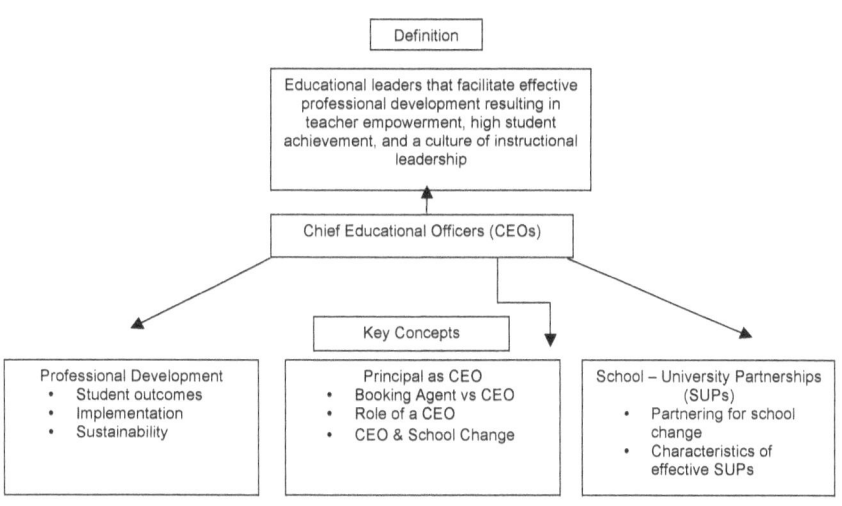

Chapter 4 Organizer

Professional development is an essential process for all educators to continue growing in their profession and improving their pedagogical expertise. Through professional development, teachers and administrators keep their licenses current, but more importantly they keep abreast of the research and best practices in education. Habitually, teachers participate in workshops and in-services to learn strategies and techniques to help them become better teachers. Typically, professional development is in the form of workshops that are disconnected. However, there are standards and research that strongly suggest that workshops alone do not change instruction. It is necessary to plan for follow-up professional development for teacher practice to change (DiPaola and Hoy 2008, 127; Marzano, Waters, and McNulty n.d., 70; Sparks and Hirsh 1997, 52).

The Learning Forward Association, formerly known as the National Staff Development Council, developed standards to shift responsibility and emphasis on learning rather than delivery (Learning Forward). The change in name of this national association is a sign of the times. No longer is professional development labeled staff development; instead, educators "learn" from professional development activities that are ongoing and job-embedded. In order to understand the process of professional development described in this book it is important to understand the standards for professional learning.

The Standards for Professional Learning (Learning Forward 2011) provide a framework that focuses on engaging educators in their own learning to improve teaching practices that result in improved student learning. The standards provide a framework for developing new skills, practices, and dispositions that impact student learning outcomes in a positive manner. The following are the Standards for Professional Learning; more detailed information may be accessed at the Professional Learning website (http://www.learningforward.org/standards/standards.cfm).

- Learning Communities: Professional learning occurs within learning communities committed to continuous improvement, collective responsibility, and goal alignment.
- Leadership: Professional learning requires skillful leaders who develop capacity, advocate, and create support systems for professional learning.
- Resources: Professional learning requires prioritizing, monitoring, and coordinating resources for educator learning.
- Data: Professional learning uses a variety of sources and types of student, educator, and system data to plan, assess, and evaluate professional learning.
- Learning Designs: Professional learning integrates theories, research, and models of human learning to achieve its intended outcomes.
- Implementation: Professional learning applies research on change and sustains support for implementation of professional learning for long-term change.
- Outcomes: Professional learning aligns its outcomes with educator performance and student curriculum standards.

The 2011 Professional Learning standards (Learning Forward 2011) set the guidelines for leading professional learning that results in improved teacher practice and student learning. Keep in mind that before any professional development is placed into action, it is essential to plan for the evaluation of the intended outcomes. Often teachers and administrators jump into implementation without planning the evaluation of an initiative or learning the research base for the implementation. Administrators are guilty of planning training because a grant funds the training, or because someone "heard" it was "a great strategy," or to spend down their professional development funding. These reasons lend themselves to scheduling one-time workshops that are engaging and interesting. The problem is that once the workshop finishes, the implementation in the classroom does not follow.

Professional development in the context of this book is defined as the ongoing learning process that takes place for teachers to practice and apply new learning into their teaching practices. This is why planning for professional development must include not only evaluating student learning but also evaluating teacher learning. The next section discusses how teacher outcomes are just as important as student outcomes.

PLANNING PROFESSIONAL DEVELOPMENT THAT IMPACTS INSTRUCTION AND LEARNING

Guskey, in his book, *Evaluating Professional Development*, emphasized the need to plan for professional development based on documented student needs (2000, 208). In order to plan for professional development, the first discussion among teachers and administrators should be centered on student learning needs.

By discussing *student* learning needs, teachers and administrators will be able to determine the desired *teacher* learning needs. For example, if students at school A are not performing at proficiency levels in Algebra 1, then teachers should look at data such as teacher-made tests, diagnostic tests, classroom observations, assessment of students' prior knowledge, etc. to determine the learning gap. Based on the findings about the learning gap, teachers and administrators collaboratively decide what instructional methods need to be used in order to address the learning gap. This is when educators should decide on the content of the professional development.

Teachers participate in the professional development and not the students, and this is why teachers' learning and practice must be included in the assessment of student outcomes. *Only after the teacher is fully imple-*

menting with fidelity can one say that the professional development helped or failed a student. In the Algebra 1 example, teachers know that students are deficient in a certain concept of Algebra 1 and therefore the intended student outcome should be that students become proficient at said concept. With this clear outcome, teachers are now able to concentrate on learning pedagogy that will help them teach the content in a manner that will enable learning and retention of the outlined outcome.

This Algebra 1 example shows how planning with an end in mind is key to focusing professional development on the real needs of students. Beginning with the end in mind is like having a GPS where teachers know their destination but need a GPS (professional development) to show them how to get to the intended destination. Professional development provides a road map with activities that include practice and feedback. As a person drives, the GPS may need to recalculate and provide modified directions based on the path the car took. Likewise, in the path of teacher learning, it is important to embed checkpoints in order to adjust and "recalculate" the next learning moment for teachers.

With all the mandates or initiatives facing schools today, such as No Child Left Behind, Race to the Top funding, and National Curriculum Standards, there is an expectation that improved student achievement results will be immediate. Teachers and principals are looking for a silver bullet that will immediately change student achievement from struggling learners to proficient. Unfortunately, change takes time and to expect immediate results is setting a professional development to fail.

There are many factors that influence the outcomes of any professional development. Here are some typical derailers: teacher's attitude, principal's attitude, resources, time, and trainer's attitude. These derailers are present at all times and therefore professional development evaluation data collection and analysis should include information about these derailers. By addressing these data, teachers and administrators are able to open communication lines and acknowledge the big picture of changing a school's culture that may result in improved student achievement.

It is important to understand that any professional development takes time to plan and then time to implement. By keeping this in mind there are several things a principal can do to help teachers:

1. Before adding a new initiative, stop and think, have teachers had enough time to implement the existing initiative(s)? If not, consider waiting to start a new one and instead allow extra time to plan for a new initiative for the following year.

2. Before adding a new initiative, stop and think, how much time do teachers have to implement on top of all the other things they are already doing? What could they stop doing to accommodate this new requirement?
3. Before adding a new initiative, stop and analyze your students' achievement data. What are the learning needs of your students and how is this new initiative going to help? What should students be doing at the end of this initiative?

Implementation is not merely letting teachers practice; there are levels of implementation that if addressed help shape the outcomes of the professional development. The point is that student outcomes can be measured and attributed to a professional development only after many factors are identified as influential to the student outcomes and are measured to determine whether they were derailers or accelerators of the student learning process. The next section describes levels of implementation of professional development.

PROFESSIONAL DEVELOPMENT AND LEVELS OF IMPLEMENTATION

Too often the authors have heard teachers say, "this too shall pass" when they sit at a workshop to learn about the latest initiative adopted by a school or school district. These initiatives are often introduced the week before school starts during "preplanning" with the expectation that teachers will immediately begin implementation, and even worse, teachers will be evaluated on this immediately!

What happens during the school year typically is that some teachers try earnestly to learn the new initiative and some try a little—usually for the scheduled evaluation observation. So much emphasis is placed on the initiatives that at the end of the year administrators look at student achievement results to determine whether an initiative works. What is wrong with this picture? There is a huge gap in professional development.

The fact that teachers were taught a new initiative does not mean that they learned it. What teachers need is time to practice and apply their new knowledge and for them to receive comprehensible feedback. Professional development is a process that requires time. It is essential to allow teachers time to learn and implement the content of a professional development. To do so, it is important to understand the levels of implementation inherent in the process of professional learning.

As discussed in the previous section, the outcomes for professional development are twofold: at the teacher level the outcome should be change in teacher practices that enhance instruction; at the student level the outcome should be change in levels of student learning. Guskey, in his book, *Evaluating Professional Development*, outlined a five-level framework that captures outcomes at the teacher implementation level and the student outcome level (2000, 79). The five levels are:

- Level 1. Participants' reactions to initial professional development;
- Level 2. Participants' learning of the content of the professional development;
- Level 3. Organizational support and change such as time, resources, and feedback while implementation is occurring;
- Level 4. Participants' use of new knowledge and skills; and
- Level 5. Student learning outcomes.

Each successive level of evaluation leads professional development planners and participants closer to the ultimate goal of impacting student learning. There are many sources of data that provide evidence of learning, implementation, support, and student outcomes. The key is to collect the data and actually analyze it to determine results. This is a problem often faced in many schools where data is overly abundant, thanks to mandated accountability systems; however, the time for analysis of the data is limited. If data is not utilized to inform instruction, then data collection becomes an exercise of storing results. Instead, data analysis should generate instructional conversations and change.

PROFESSIONAL DEVELOPMENT AND SUSTAINABILITY

There are many professional developments that do "stick" in schools. Some professional developments become engrained in how the school functions and are sustained over time. How are these professional developments different than the rest? First, principals and teachers understand that change takes time (Hord, Rutherford, and Huling-Austin 1987, 5). Therefore, if professional development is going to impact teacher practice, there needs to be a plan in place that allows for implementation, coaching, feedback, and reflection (Joyce and Showers 1996, 12).

Joyce and Showers in their seminal research in the 1980s, "Improving Inservice Training: Messages from Research," concluded that teachers who implemented new practices into their teaching were those who participated in professional development that included ongoing, job-embedded feedback and reflection. In their two-year study they found that direct coaching provided by peers, supervisors, professors, or others was necessary to apply new learning into their lessons (1980, 384). Sixteen years after publishing their research, Joyce and Showers in "The Evolution of Peer Coaching" reported that peer coaching when practiced regularly, and by regularly they mean on a weekly basis, resulted in teachers implementing new learning into their teaching (1996, 15). They go on to advocate for setting up peer coaching teams from the first day of school.

Peer coaching in teams is a research-based practice that changes instruction. In order to implement a strategy such as peer coaching teams, there needs to be visionary school principals who are knowledgeable in professional development and are willing to envision their schools as giant learning places. This means that the principals see themselves as teachers and the principals' students are the teachers in the building. This idea is not explicitly taught to principals in their principal preparation programs. Principal preparation programs traditionally prepare principals to manage a school and thus the approach to professional development is that of a booking agent.

BOOKING AGENT VS. CEO

This book refers to principals who "book" a professional development act as booking agent. A booking agent typically selects engaging presenters for their teachers to learn from (O'Neal and Ringler 2013, 2). The booking agent then makes sure that the act has the appropriate materials needed for the presentation, including technology, comfortable seating, snacks, and handouts. Booking agents also take the tickets at the door, making sure that all teachers are present and sign in for the "act." Once the "act" is introduced, the booking agent principal leaves the room to tend to other administrative matters.

The booking agent principal contracts with an external consultant to deliver workshops or provide in-service activities with the purpose of developing teachers' expertise. The idea of developing teachers professionally is valuable; however, with the booking agent it often fails because the principal has done nothing more than book the act, book the room, and sell the tickets to the event. The booking agent's lack of engagement beyond the planning phase negatively impacts the teachers' perception that learning is important because if it were important then the principal should be present and learn what is being taught.

In contrast, the Chief Education Officer (CEO) principal plans for outcomes and processes with the external consultant and teachers. The workshops and in-service activities are the beginning of the change process. The change process takes time and practice. The CEO facilitates the follow-up process, supporting teachers by providing time to plan, time to collaborate, and most importantly time for peer coaching and peer observation (O'Neal and Ringler 2013, 4). It is the creative blending of the principal, teacher, and consultant that develops an atmosphere of trust and professional growth.

CEO AND SCHOOL CHANGE

The Concerns-Based Adoption Model (CBAM) (Hord, Rutherford, and Huling-Austin 1987) is a model developed at the Research and Development Center for Teacher Education at the University of Texas at Austin that is widely accepted and often mentioned on the topic of change in schools. CBAM is an empirically based conceptual framework that outlined the development process that teachers experienced as they implemented an innovation. The research for this model was based on many years of intensive school-based research on the change process as a whole, with special emphasis on implementation of innovations in schools and colleges. Findings of this model yielded six basic assumptions about change and how it is best facilitated (Hord, Rutherford, and Huling-Austin 1987, 5).

The six assumptions about change (table 4.1) were carefully considered by the ongoing professional development, which is the basis of this book. The authors of the book facilitated professional development on a weekly basis at a rural elementary, middle, and high school in eastern North Carolina. Teachers received ongoing and sustained professional development via weekly observations, feedback, collaborative planning, and workshops. The authors found that the frequent visits and the comprehensible feedback significantly accelerated the rate of implementation of a research-based instructional model that focused on academic language literacy (ALL); see chapter 2 for a complete explanation of ALL.

Change is a process that involves teachers' affective and cognitive needs. In order to facilitate change, there needs to be a visionary that sets the

Table 4.1. CBAM Change Process in Professional Development

CBAM Change Process	CBAM Findings	Project CEO Findings
Change is a process, not an event.	It is a process that occurs over time, usually over a period of several years.	Teachers agreed that learning a new model takes time and effort. The first year was a time to practice and learn.
Individuals accomplish change.	Change affects people, and their role in the process of change is very important.	Teachers' practice changed when *each* teacher in the project successfully implemented the new model focusing on ALL.
Change is a highly personal experience.	Each individual reacts differently to change.	Some teachers incorporated the new model in their teaching faster than others. Individual feedback on implementation was essential.
Change entails multilevel developmental growth.	Each individual demonstrates growth in terms of their acquisition of skills and their positive feelings.	As teachers increased their experiences with the new model, their skills and attitudes tended to improve.
Change is best understood in operational terms.	Individuals relate to change in terms of what it means to them or how it affects their situation.	The project succinctly addressed teachers' concerns. The most common concerns of lack of time and resources were addressed by providing an assistant and stipends for time commitments outside their teaching contracts.
Change focuses on individuals, innovations, and context.	The real focus is on the individuals, not on the new curriculum or the new program.	The focus of the project was on the teachers' concerns and their learning of the new model.

destination and then facilitates the travel to the destination. School leaders that make teacher development and student learning their priority facilitate successful change. This type of school leader is what this book labels a Chief Education Officer or CEO.

PRINCIPAL AS CEO

A CEO realizes that teacher development is accomplished one teacher at a time. An effective CEO believes that professional development is a positive way to improve teacher practice. An effective CEO implements professional development that is systemic, frequent, and high quality. Systemic professional development has a two-dimensional goal: to improve student learning and to improve teacher learning. Principals who successfully implement professional development have fully developed plans that include ongoing opportunities for teachers to practice, to receive feedback, and to reflect on implementation (Lindstrom and Speck 2004, 18). In addition to having a well-conceived plan, an effective CEO is deeply engaged and involved in the professional development by actively participating in all workshops. Active participation sends a message that "this professional development is important and I am learning this with you."

Systemic professional development is transparent in nature. A CEO in collaboration with teachers develops a schedule of activities that includes dates and times for teachers to plan ahead. The activities should scaffold teachers' learning. In the professional development research that is the basis for this book (referred to as Project CEO from this point forward), the schedule of activities included learning one new component each month so that by the end of the school year teachers were implementing all the components of the model. Additional scaffolding occurred by reviewing the past month's component before learning a new component at the first meeting each month.

The next activity of Project CEO was to schedule collaborative planning times so that teachers could discuss their new learning and incorporation of new strategies in their lessons. After planning, teachers were expected to conduct peer observations and engage in a peer feedback process. In Project CEO, principals worked collaboratively with the authors, two experts from a local university. The principals and the authors scheduled monthly collaborative planning times to discuss the progress of professional development, teacher learning, and barriers and successes, and to plan meaningful monthly activities.

Frequent professional development refers not to how many times teachers meet for training but to how often teachers engage in meaningful instructional conversations about their practice. There are a variety of ways to foster development around teacher practice. Examples are peer coaching, lesson study groups, collaborative planning, and comprehensible feedback. Sparks and Hirsh share that the most powerful professional development is teachers talking with other teachers about student work and comparing it to standards (1997, 41). In Project CEO, teachers reported that their most valued feedback was the feedback that principals provided about their teaching. Teachers felt that principals understood their stressors, challenges, and successes.

A CEO is able to facilitate instructional dialogue with the purpose of locating an intended destination—this also provides a blueprint for evaluating the success or failure of the professional development that leads to the destination. The earlier Algebra 1 example is an ideal situation where teachers and the CEO together decide on professional development; however, in many schools professional development is mandated as opposed to self-selected. There are many reasons for the professional development mandates and what an effective CEO does is to show the teachers how the "new initiative" fits within the school's needs. If there is not a fit then that becomes a discussion between the CEO and the school district; however, if the professional development is based on research there is a strong possibility that there is a positive correlation between school need and current mandate.

Table 4.2 outlines characteristics of principals as booking agents or CEOs. Next time a professional development opportunity arises, principals could use this table to follow CEO instructional leadership and avoid the potential of "wasting" time and resources by acting like booking agents.

SCHOOL-UNIVERSITY PARTNERSHIPS

With all the demands on schools to prepare college-ready students, principals have their hands full and their time is committed to their buildings. An effective way to bring innovation to a school is to form professional development partnerships with universities. Universities can help principals and schools by providing resources such as content knowledge, pedagogical expertise, coaching support, and monetary resources. University professors are an excellent source of help.

In Project CEO, two professors wrote a grant that brought expertise, resources, and ongoing coaching to three schools. In the case of Project CEO, two years of professional development resulted in developing teacher leaders and helping improve student achievement. The work of Project CEO also generated research that informs educational practice and principal preparation. School-university partnerships and networks ensure that cur-

Table 4.2. Booking Agent vs. CEO

	CEO	Booking Agent
What is the purpose of the professional development?	• Needed due to data analysis. • PLC decided that they would like to implement. • Fits with school improvement goals or strategic goals. • Fits with current initiatives.	• Mandate from district office. • Need to spend down budget. • Went to a training and the presenter was excellent. • Nearby school district is doing this.
What are the expected outcomes? (How will you know it worked?)	• There is a plan for collecting teacher implementation data. • Time is allotted for implementation of at least one year before formal evaluation.	• Student achievement should increase—ASAP. • Student achievement data is the only measure of success.
How will the professional development be delivered?	• There is a plan for ongoing professional development that includes PLCs and peer coaching. • Principal schedules observations and feedback sessions.	• Training scheduled for pre-planning. • Training scheduled for teacher professional development days. • No expectations for weekly implementation except for trainings.
Who will do the training?	• Trainers provide opportunities to practice skills. • Training is engaging and hands-on.	• Lectures or boring presenter. • Participants are not engaged in the learning process.
What support is needed?	• Principal prepared to provide feedback often. • Principal commits to finding time for teachers to plan, observe, and learn. • Principal finds resources to support lesson plans.	• Principal plans to observe during the official evaluation time. • There is no money for resources. • Time to learn is not addressed.

rent research is shared as well as provide the opportunity to participate in generating new research-based information (Lindstrom and Speck 2004, 66).

In Project CEO one university professor was from the College of Arts and Sciences and provided the expertise in linguistics and ESL teacher education. She taught ESL in public schools and taught in the ESL licensure program at East Carolina University. The SIOP® developers trained Ms. O'Neal and she, in turn, trained the second university professor who worked on Project CEO. Dr. Ringler is a professor in Educational Leadership who has worked with national experts of professional development and continues to research effective professional development through her work with educational leadership. Both professors have presented workshops on integrating language and content across the curriculum to various mainstream teacher groups, emphasizing the classroom teacher's role in content literacy instruction and the principal's role in facilitating implementation.

Both worked together providing SIOP® professional development to rural school districts in eastern North Carolina and have also co-presented their work at various national, state, and regional conferences. A precursor professional development project to Project CEO took place in rural Sampson county with two high-poverty, high-ELL elementary schools. The results of that research empowered teachers to become leaders while improving their instruction. The principals in these two schools were CEOs prior to working with the authors. The collaborative partnership among the principals and the authors identified the important role a principal has in facilitating implementation of new instructional strategies through sustained school-university partnership (Lys, Ringler, and O'Neal 2009, 6).

Partnering for School Change

Through ongoing professional development in rural eastern North Carolina and ongoing reflection among the different school leaders, "it became evident that the consistent ongoing and objective input from the university faculty was a motivating factor for the continuation of efforts at the school level" (Lys, Ringler, and O'Neal 2009, 7). The school-university partners who have promoted school change were those who engaged both university professors and school administrators and teachers in an ongoing learning community about academic language literacy.

Effective partnerships first agreed at both the district and school level to participate in ongoing professional development. After a clear understanding of the goals of the professional development, the school-university partners collaborated to create workable timelines, strategies, and evaluation processes for their schools.

The key to partnering for school change is to trust each other's areas of expertise and understanding that all involved in the partnership are engaged in their own professional growth for the betterment of students. University experts grow professionally because they are not engrained in the day-to-day activities of a school and therefore rely on school administrators and teachers to interpret the content and apply it to their context. School administrators and teachers do not have the time to learn new content and continue with their daily responsibilities and therefore rely on the university experts to learn and deliver the content of the professional development.

Partnering for school change also provides an opportunity for teachers to grow professionally in their instructional leadership potential. Through the years that the authors have partnered with schools, it has been evident that teachers often feel like "subordinates" more than professionals. Some examples of "subordinate" behaviors found by the authors include:

- Teachers often expect to be told what to do;
- Teachers often expect to be given a script or outline to follow;
- Teachers often worry that changing their lesson plans may result in negative evaluations;
- Teachers worry that if principals walk into their classroom and hear "a noisy classroom" that this may negatively reflect in their evaluations;
- Teachers often express defensive attitudes when ALL strategies are introduced because they feel that their teaching effectiveness is being criticized.

During long-term professional development in school-university partnerships, teachers are provided opportunities to contribute as professionals, use academic language and strategies to orally communicate their ideas, and practice, apply, critique, and provide feedback in a safe learning environment. All of these ongoing and frequent opportunities have resulted in developing/finding teachers' professional voices, developing teacher leaders, and most importantly becoming better teachers of academic language of their content.

Characteristics of Effective School-University Partnerships

Educational institutions at the K–12 and higher education levels cannot exist on their own; without partnerships among universities and local school districts, there is no educational research. However, in order for meaningful partnerships to flourish there must be a perceived value and expectation of meaningful results for all partners (O'Neal, Ringler, and Lys 2009, 52). Project CEO's collaborative partnership brought together a variety of stakeholders from the university, from the district office, and from the schools with the common goal of achieving high levels of teacher implementation of academic language literacy. Several characteristics were present in this effective school-university partnership.

Common Goal. The goal of a school-university partnership should be clearly articulated. In Project CEO the goal was to implement academic language literacy (ALL) strategies in elementary schools in a rural county in eastern North Carolina. The goal clearly indicated that the ALL model would give teachers the necessary skills to teach content while simultaneously focusing on academic language development. The goal also indicated that principals would gain the necessary skills to become CEOs. Clarifying and understanding the goal is key to the success of a partnership. Before jumping into activities, the partners should meet to clarify, agree, and put in writing the professional development goals.

Stakeholders. Partnership between schools and universities should involve professionals who are invested in children's education above all. University faculty should be invested in providing a service and researching their service work to inform professional practice. Often the authors heard from school stakeholders their perception that university faculty often wanted to engage in their personal research and "take" opportunities for their own learning, but this research often did not provide benefits for the school, students, teachers, or administrators. This form of partnership is one-sided and leaves the school partners feeling "used."

An effective partnership should be mutually beneficial and therefore faculty may publish their research from their work with schools; however, the work with the schools should meet the schools' educational needs and be mutually defined by stakeholders from the university and the schools.

The school partners need to include district-level leadership, principals, and a team of teachers. In Project CEO the district was rural and small and therefore the partners were the superintendent, principals, and a team of teachers. In other districts the authors have teamed with directors of federal programs, directors of professional development, principals, instructional coaches, and teams of teachers.

There are many layers of collaboration for which each of the stakeholders take responsibility; typically university partners are instrumental in collaborating with the district level to facilitate the planning and financing of the professional development workshops and ongoing yearly activities. The university faculty members provide the content and work directly with the principals to plan the follow-up meetings and peer coaching sessions. Teachers engage in practice and application as well as peer coaching.

Buy-in. It is important to obtain commitment to the partnership and professional development goals. The "buy-in" must be created not only among the teachers, but also between the teachers and their principals, the principals and the district-level administrators, and finally the school personnel with the university faculty. The "buy-in" should be evident through action of the stakeholders and this is where the CEO skills shine. CEOs prioritize the partnership and therefore make time to be present in the professional development activities. Promises, activities, and challenges are dealt with and followed through. Therefore, open communication among stakeholders is key to a successful ongoing "buy-in."

Creating a Learning Community. A learning community should instill professional growth in all members as well as nurture a sense of collegiality and leadership. In Project CEO the authors sensed that many of the federal and state mandates have taken professionalism away from teachers. Project CEO inspired and reenergized teachers to continue their professional growth. The learning community gave them pride in their teaching skills and a venue to implement innovations in teaching and learning.

A learning community should be a forum for celebration and honest discussions. It is important to showcase successes among school staff. Often errors and negative situations steal the spotlight in schools. CEOs and the learning community are responsible for publicly highlighting instances of ALL, both positive and those that provide opportunity for learning. The learning community stakeholders should include time to decide on important accomplishments to be shared, and the teachers and administrators should do the sharing.

As the learning community evolves, so should the level of learning and professional activities. Project CEO participants presented at two national conferences: one for teachers of ALL and another for educational leaders. At these national conferences, teachers and administrators presented their work with Project CEO and thus added a dimension of leadership in their profession.

Long-term Commitment to Professional Development. Professional development that results in change in teacher practice takes time to implement; therefore, the learning community needs to agree to a long-term commitment of implementation with constant feedback on implementation. With this understanding, the planning of the professional development is essential and should be allowed time to plan before implementing. Project CEO delivered an initial professional development as an intensive immersion where the learning community blocked two and a half days during the summer. This intensive professional development provided an overview and research of what was to be implemented during the year.

The yearlong implementation involved weekly coaching sessions, monthly principals' meetings, and weekly implementation activities for teachers. The implementation activities are described in chapter 5. By maintaining ongoing communication and activities on a weekly basis between the school and the university faculty, the professional development was maintained as a priority.

SUMMARY

Professional development is a healthy source of change in schools. If disjointed and disconnected professional development is sprinkled in schools, it is unlikely that instruction and student achievement will be affected as desired. No system of interventions can compensate for weak and ineffective teaching (DuFour et al. 2010, 39). Professional learning communities are a form of professional development that integrates ongoing professional development—key to changing teacher practice. Principals who are CEOs must be committed to improving the professional practice of teachers individually and collectively.

One of the key messages in this book is that an effective principal is a CEO who embraces professional development as a strategy to improve instruction and improve student learning. In order to do so, teachers must collaborate and learn together on a daily basis with the purpose of improving their instruction. Studying their content and the way to teach their content in ways that improve student learning involves peer collaboration. CEOs have instructional leadership skills that encourage teachers to engage in learning, implementing, and reflecting.

A CEO needs a coordinated professional development plan that is developed in collaboration with teachers and university partners. The goal is to focus on academic language learning as a means to teaching content. Content teachers need ongoing and job-embedded professional development to learn how to teach the content using academic language strategies. The use of language as evidence of learning will be developed in the next chapter.

WORKS CITED

DiPaola, Michael F., and Wayne K. Hoy. *Principals Improving Instruction: Supervision, Evaluation and Professional Development*. Boston: Pearson Education, 2008.

DuFour, Richard, Rebecca DuFour, Robert Eaker, and Gayle Karhanek. *Raising the Bar and Closing the Achievement Gap*. Bloomington: Solution Tree, 2010.

Guskey, Thomas. *Evaluating Professional Development*. Thousand Oaks: Corwin, 2000.

Hord, Shirley M., William L. Rutherford, and Leslie Huling-Austin. *Taking Charge of Change*. Austin: Southwest Educational Development Laboratory, 1987.

Joyce, Bruce, and Beverly Showers. "Improving Inservice Training: The Messages of Research." *Educational Leadership* 37.5 (1980): 379–85.

———. "The Evolution of Peer Coaching." *Educational Leadership* 56.6 (1996): 12–16.

Learning Forward. *Standards for Professional Learning*. Oxford: OH. Author, 2011. Web source.

Lindstrom, Phyllis H., and Marsha Speck. *The Principal as a Professional Development Leader*. Thousand Oaks: Corwin, 2004.

Lys, Diana, Marjorie Ringler, and Debra O'Neal. "Changing Teacher Attitudes Toward Instruction of Academic Language Through Sustained School-University Partnership." *International Journal of Educational Leadership Preparation* 4.4 (2009): 1–7.

Marzano, Robert J., Timothy Waters, and Brian A McNulty. *School Leadership that Works: From Research to Results*. Alexandria: Association for Supervision and Curriculum Development, n.d.

O'Neal, Debra, and Marjorie Ringler. "From Booking Agent to CEO." *Principal Leadership (NASSP)*, February 14, 2013. Accessed August 5, 2014. www.nassp.org/PL0213oneal.

O'Neal, Debra, Marjorie C. Ringler, and Diana Lys. "Skeptics to Partners: University Teams with District to Improve ELL Instruction." *Journal of Staff Development* 30.4 (2009): 52–55.

Sparks, Dennis, and Stephanie Hirsh. *A New Vision for Staff Development*. Alexandria: Association for Supervision and Curriculum Development, 1997.

5

IMPLEMENTING SUSTAINABLE PROFESSIONAL DEVELOPMENT

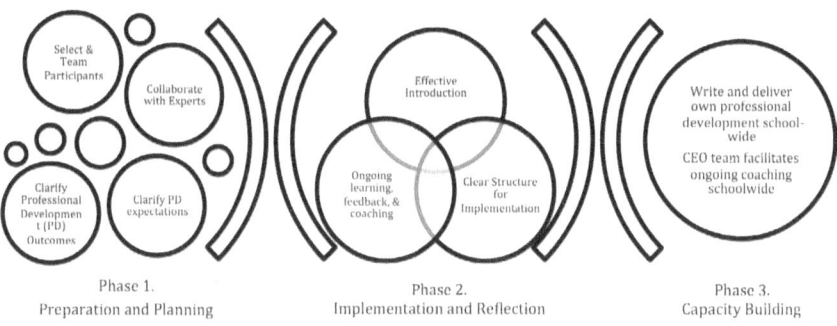

Chapter 5 Organizer

Chapter 4 describes national standards that should guide professional development if it is going to be implemented as a tool to improve teaching and learning. The standards developed by Learning Forward (2011) emphasize that professional development should be job-embedded and abundant of ongoing feedback and coaching. This chapter provides a practical and concrete manner to implement professional development that results in implementation that changes teaching and learning as it builds capacity to sustain teacher development.

The examples provided in this chapter are a result of years of implementation and research with various rural school districts in eastern North

Carolina. The leadership standard for professional learning (Learning Forward 2011) requires skillful leaders who develop capacity, advocate, and create support systems for professional learning. This chapter provides school leaders a framework and a practical process to implement in schools.

Chapter 4 explained why professional development in the context of this book is defined as the ongoing learning process that takes place for teachers to practice and apply new learning into their teaching practices on an ongoing basis. This book proposes that planning for professional development must include not only assessing student learning but also assessing teacher learning. In fact, before evaluating teacher learning, professional development should provide ample opportunities for teachers to practice and learn.

Time for learning means pausing formal summative evaluation of the new practice to make way for formative evaluations that provide feedback on implementation with a feeling of safety and professionalism. Teachers need to know that they have time to try new things and that they have time to learn from their implementation before they are expected to "know" everything about the implementation—a practice that is not common in education. Often teachers are sent to training and are expected to train other teachers about what they learned before teachers themselves implement and learn from their implementation. What is missing here?

This train the trainer practice (without time to implement before training) is like trying to fly a plane after using a flight simulator for many hours. Sure the person knows what they are supposed to do because the simulator taught them the theory and the skills to fly a plane, but the actual flying of a plane is what will be the telling factor in whether you know how to fly safely. Every person learning how to fly takes lessons with a flight instructor before flying their own plane without supervision, right? Often teachers are sent to learn to fly at a professional development (simulator experiences) and then are asked to teach others to fly (flight instructor) without even flying a plane for themselves. There is a major learning step missing (flying lessons)! This chapter provides a framework for teacher-learning time that includes formative feedback to ensure that the professional development is implemented with fidelity.

Once instructional leaders assess that professional development is being implemented as it should, then they can study student-learning outcomes as a measure of the professional development effectiveness. However, this book recognizes the accountability need to measure student-learning outcomes and therefore recommends measuring student baseline data and also analyzing pre- and post-student work samples, as well as attitudinal and affective measures about student learning as part of the formative assessments.

Before the framework is described, it is important to reiterate that selecting the content of the professional development is a process that should be considered carefully based on the student-learning needs of the school and the teaching strategies necessary to address the student-learning needs (Guskey 2000, 36). An instructional leader, collaboratively with teachers, needs to be clear and committed to addressing a student-learning need and use these data to determine what professional development teachers need to strengthen instruction to improve student learning.

Often the content of the professional development is mandated by the school district's central administration. If a mandate is the spur for professional development, then it is essential to develop a crosswalk or alignment of the new professional development and how it satisfies educational needs of the school and how it aligns with the existing initiatives at the school. Table 5.1 provides a crosswalk developed by Project CEO collaboratively between the authors of the book and the principal and teachers of a rural high school. This crosswalk helped the high school staff make the decision to learn a new professional development that complemented their ongoing work with an existing initiative.

Project CEO was based on a model of building capacity of teacher leaders who are able to translate the professional development practices into practice, resulting in improved teaching and student learning in the classroom (Sparks and Hirsh 1997, 4). The framework in this chapter is generic to any professional development content. However, it will only work if the professional development is relevant to the student-learning needs of the school. In addition, Project CEO adapted related literature on the vision for staff development (Darling-Hammond 1996; Guskey 2000; Joyce and Showers 1998) into a three-phase model for professional development (see table 1.1):

Phase One: Preparation and Planning;
Phase Two: Implementation & Reflection; and
Phase Three: Capacity Building.

A complete description of each phase is included in the sections that follow.

Even though the professional development is generic, this book utilized this framework and conducted research about academic language literacy (ALL). Therefore, the framework described below provides a concrete model for ALL professional development.

Table 5.1. Sample Initiative Crosswalk for Professional Development Integration

SIOP® STRATEGIES	CIF ELEMENTS
Teacher Preparation 1. Teachers write clearly defined content objectives on the board for students. These objectives are reviewed at the beginning of a lesson; students should state at the end of the lesson whether the objectives have been met. 2. Teachers should write clearly defined language objectives on the board for students at the beginning of a lesson. Students state at the end of the lesson whether the objectives have been met. 3. Concepts taught should be appropriate for the age and educational background of students. Teachers must consider the students' L1 literacy, second language proficiency, and the reading level of the materials. 4. Supplementary materials are used to promote comprehension. These include charts, graphs, pictures, illustrations, regalia, math manipulatives, multimedia, and demonstrations by teacher and other students. 5. Content must be adapted to ELL's needs through use of graphic organizers, outlines, labeling of pictures, study guides, adapted text, and highlighted text. 6. Meaningful activities integrate lesson concepts with language practice opportunities in listening, speaking, reading, and writing.	Scaffolding Writing to Learn Collaborative Group Work Classroom Talk Literacy Groups
Building Background 1. Concepts should be directly linked to students' background experience. This experience can be personal, cultural, or academic. 2. Links should be explicitly made between past learning and new concepts. 3. Key vocabulary is emphasized. New vocabulary is presented in context. The number of vocabulary items is limited.	Scaffolding Classroom Talk Writing to Learn
Comprehensible Input 1. Use speech that is appropriate for students' language proficiency. 2. Make the explanation of the task clear using step-by-step manner with visuals. 3. Use of a variety of techniques to make content concepts clear. Teachers need to focus attention selectively on the most important information. Introduce new learning in context. Help students learn strategies such as predicting and summarizing.	Scaffolding Writing to Learn Questioning Classroom Talk

PHASE ONE: PREPARATION AND PLANNING

Phase one focuses on developing the principal and school leaders into CEO teams. The professional development activities in this phase teach the CEO team academic literacy in the content areas to become competent in application of the research-based ALL strategies. The goal of phase one is to provide the CEO team an overview of how to fully integrate academic language instruction and content-area instruction.

An initial professional development establishes the protocols and procedures for the yearlong learning community. The preparation and planning phase develops the plan for implementation. The following are key aspects of phase one.

Collaborate with Experts of ALL and Professional Development

In phase one, CEOs should avail themselves of experts in the content of the professional development who also have expertise in delivering ongoing, job-embedded professional development. The CEO should take this opportunity to learn the skills that the experts bring and develop partnerships for ongoing collaboration. In chapter 4 the book explains the importance of developing school-university partnerships for this purpose. Selecting experts for partnership is an important process. The partners should not only be experts in their content areas but also exhibit effective interpersonal skills with experience working with the change process with teachers and administrators. In Project CEO, the university experts were two faculty members, one from the College of Education, Department of Educational Leadership and one from the College of Arts and Sciences, Department of English. Their roles were essential in developing the framework for professional development and providing learning and coaching structures in this project.

Dr. Ringler's role was to facilitate the principal development and leadership roles within the project. Principal learning and teacher learning resulted in a change in instruction, focusing more on student-centered strategies. In conducting their school-wide meetings, the principals also applied the ALL strategies, resulting in more engaged instructional conversations. In addition, Dr. Ringler was responsible for collecting and analyzing project data to inform the yearlong process.

Ms. O'Neal's role was to integrate the linguistic component into the content areas. She was also responsible for gathering appropriate supplementary materials and engaging national experts for the monthly meetings and weekly visits. She facilitated the participation of the group at a national conference for teachers of English as a second language. Ms. O'Neal worked directly with content teachers, guiding pedagogy to focus on language in the classroom, resulting in transforming content teachers to language teachers of content.

Together, the university experts used the ALL model to deliver professional development and promote academic language proficiency. In chapter 2 the book described several models that provide ALL strategies. During phase one, Project CEO provided a sampling of the content of the professional development and also an opportunity to experience what it was like to work with the experts by offering a shortened two-hour workshop. This workshop also helped the school district understand the content of the project better. Textbox 5.1 and table 5.2 provide an example of a brief workshop agenda helpful to learn more about ALL professional development.

Textbox 5.1. Sample Phase I Workshop

Deciphering Academic Language
Recommended length of training: two hours
Workshop goals:
- To create a common understanding of the terms: linguistic diversity, academic language proficiency, dialectal variations, code-switching, BICS and CALP (Cummins 1984)
- To build background for the follow-up sessions on strategies for developing academic language proficiency across the content areas

Desired Outcomes: Participants will become aware of linguistic diversity and will focus their instruction to improve academic language proficiency for ALL students by:
- Creating more engaged classrooms
- Moving from lecture-based instruction to participatory, engaged learning

Table 5.2. Sample Phase I Workshop

WHAT (content)	HOW	WHO	TIME (minutes)
Welcome/Start-Ups • Purpose/Context • Desired Outcomes • Agenda	Present Q & A Agreement	CEO	5
Redefining Linguistic Diversity • Presentation • Interactive Activities	Present Discuss Q & A Clarify	Linguistic and Professional Development Experts	50
BREAK		**ALL**	10
What Is Academic Language • Presentation • Interactive Activities	Present Discuss Q & A Clarify	Linguistic Expert and Professional Development Expert	45
Homework • Articles to read	Present Discuss Q & A Clarify	Linguistic Expert and Professional Development Expert	5
Evaluation +/-	Record	CEO	5

Select CEO Team Participants

In phase one, an important decision for the CEO is to select the professional development participants or the CEO team. The goal is for participating teachers to integrate ALL strategies into all content areas and to develop into instructional leaders. In the authors' years of research, they have found that starting small and then expanding to school-wide implementation works best. Starting with a small group of participants allows time to build relationships between professional developers and the school as well as time to work out details that are specific to the school context. Also, the small group of initial implementers tends to become the instructional leaders in the professional development content.

In the authors' experience, a group of twenty or fewer is a good size. How should the CEO select the small group? CEOs should consider creating a team of teachers who:

1. Represent each grade level in elementary school or a core content in secondary schools.
2. Are genuinely interested in improving their teaching skills. The authors have found that selected teachers need to know why they were selected. The authors always inform the CEO team that they were selected for their willingness to learn and that there is not a perception that their teaching is in need of improvement due to poor performance.

    The authors often assure them that their teaching experiences are considered effective and that the professional development is meant to provide them with strategies that they can add to their repertoire of instructional strategies. And this is true! If professional development is going to be effective, the judgment factor needs to be eliminated and replaced with instructional dialogue about teaching and learning. The use of reflection and peer coaching is essential to keep conversations about teaching and learning to a professional level and not a personal level.
3. Exhibit teacher leadership potential. Some teachers have some inherent leadership potential as they are required to work with mainstream teachers and share instructional strategies related to the students' linguistic or cognitive learning needs. These roles are found in instructional coaches or specialists such as ESL or special education teachers.

Note that not all teachers exhibit leadership potential, but that potential may be awakened by a positive professional development experience.

Ultimately, CEO principals need to decide whom they want to participate in the professional development based on their knowledge of their teaching staff. There could be a combination of reasons including teacher leaders, marginal teachers, naysayers, or content-specific teachers (e.g., math only or language arts only). Regardless of who is selected, it is important that the teachers selected understand the reasons for their selection, the content of the professional development, and the time requirements.

Once teachers are recruited and selected, CEO principals need to pair teachers into learning teams. These learning teams will be required to engage in weekly instructional dialogue, observe each other, and provide each other implementation feedback. In Project CEO, principals paired elementary teachers with middle school teachers the first year and then middle school teachers with high school teachers the second year. As much as possible, the principals tried matching content areas; however, it was possible to team non-content alike teachers and still provide feedback on the academic language strategies.

The principals at each school had an active role in the CEO team; therefore, each principal teamed with a teacher. When their teacher needed to observe, they both observed a third teacher in the team and then engaged in coaching and dialogue together.

Table 5.3 shows the learning teams developed through Project CEO between the elementary school and the middle school. In this project, the elementary school teachers decided to focus on academic language literacy (ALL) in mathematics and the middle school teachers focused on ALL in each content area. This focus provided common ground for content language dialogue. The principal of the elementary school was a former science teacher and therefore chose to work with the middle school science teacher. The middle school principal chose to work with a teacher who was a veteran teacher and set in her ways. The middle school principal saw this professional development as an opportunity to promote change in this teacher, who would be more resistant to change than others.

Table 5.4 shows the learning teams developed through Project CEO between the middle school and the high school. These sets of teams were implemented during the second year of work at this rural school district. The CEO middle school teachers consisted of the teacher leaders who emerged from the previous yearlong implementation.

The fact that the CEO middle school teachers had a year's worth of implementation was beneficial to the success of this project because they helped build trust and convince high school teachers of the value of focusing on ALL. High school teachers are unique because they see themselves

Table 5.3. CEO Elementary and Middle School Teams

CEO Elementary School	CEO Middle School
Principal	Seventh and eighth grade Science teacher
Kindergarten teacher	Sixth grade Math teacher
First grade teacher	Sixth grade English teacher
Second grade teacher	Sixth grade Science teacher
Third grade teacher	Seventh and eighth grade Math teacher
Fourth grade teacher	Seventh and eighth grade Social Studies teacher
Fifth grade teacher	Principal

Table 5.4. CEO Middle and High School Team

CEO Middle School	CEO High School
Principal	Principal
Math teacher (sixth grade)	Algebra teacher
Math teacher (seventh and eighth grade)	History teacher
Social Studies teacher (sixth grade)	Civics teacher
English teacher (seventh and eighth grade)	Computer teacher
English teacher (sixth grade)	English teacher
ESL teacher (sixth–twelfth grade)	Earth Space Science teacher
Science teacher (seventh and eighth grade)	Computer teacher

as content experts and therefore asking them to focus on pedagogical strategies that focused on ALL is more general than they are used to. In the authors' experience, high school teachers equate ALL only with content vocabulary and as described in chapter 2, ALL is much more that teaching content vocabulary. In addition, the high school was successfully implementing a different initiative and required several sessions of professional dialogue to develop a crosswalk document (see table 5.1) to illustrate that the ALL strategies complemented and integrated all the great work they had accomplished at the time the project started at their school.

Once the teams are selected, it is important to clarify the professional development outcomes and the concrete demands of the teachers' time.

Clarify Professional Development Outcomes

Professional development outcomes should be clearly described in terms of goals and objectives that reflect the documented need for improvement. For ALL, the goals and objectives should be supported by content-intensive instruction, explicit instruction and modeling of effective coaching, and follow-up strategies. These goals and objectives promote implementation via learning communities and redefinition of the school leadership goals to enable ongoing sustainable professional development, resulting in schoolwide implementation of ALL strategies.

The goals and objectives become a tool for planning and then can be used for evaluating the effectiveness of the professional development. Table 5.5 illustrates how Project CEO utilized Guskey's levels of professional development evaluation as a framework for implementation of ALL (Guskey 2000, 79). Note that experts in ALL and professional development delivery should deliver the content of the professional development.

Table 5.5. Planning and Evaluation of ALL Professional Development

Professional Development Goal	Objectives	Alignment with Guskey's professional development evaluation	Evidence
Increase teachers' knowledge and pedagogical skills in teaching academic language of their content	Teachers understand the ALL model and its components	Level of knowledge and level of implementation	Pre- and post-test Lesson plans
Provide sustained high-quality professional development when coaching and providing follow-up ALL activities to improve content area achievement	Practice ongoing coaching skills to provide feedback on implementation Implement ALL on a daily basis in classrooms Monthly reflections Increase student achievement in content areas	Level of organization support Level of implementation Level of student outcomes	Conference-observation-conference minutes Lesson plans Reflective journals Evidence of student achievement growth scores
Enhance CEO leaders' skills as instructional leaders	Provide leadership and organizational support for high-quality ongoing professional development	Level of organizational support	Interviews of teachers and instructional leaders
CEO leaders deliver high-quality professional development school-wide after own yearlong implementation is completed using materials and experiences developed during the year.	Reflect on yearlong experiences and develop own professional development to the rest of the school staff using materials and experiences from previous year Develop an implementation timeline and follow-up activities for school-wide implementation	Level of implementation	Professional development evaluation Level of school-wide implementation: lesson plans and observations

In the planning phase, understanding the goals of the professional development and the outcome measures are important. Often these goals are understood more clearly by the school administration; the CEO's job responsibilities often deal with outcomes and measures. For teachers, understanding these goals may take more time. In the authors' experience and consistent with change theory, participating teachers in this phase are concerned about what this professional development translates to in terms of concrete expectations of the teachers' time and end product (Hord, Rutherford, and Huling-Austin 1987, 44). For this reason, it is important to dedicate a planning meeting early in the professional development (the authors recommend the initial meeting) to clarify time expectations. Textbox 5.2 provides a sample agenda for this initial meeting.

The authors have found that clarifying monthly expectations helps. For the professional development framework described in this book, a set of activities is planned on a monthly basis and then the activities repeat themselves with a change in the content per month—always including time to review previous learning and making connections between previous learning and new learning. The framework requires five main expectations.

Expectation 1. The content of the professional development will be implemented in the classroom. For Project CEO, the expectation was that ALL strategies be implemented on a daily basis and that teachers would modify their lesson plans monthly to include components of the professional development as they learn them. The authors found that teachers prefer using their own lesson planning models and that they find their own

Textbox 5.2. Sample Initial Team Building Agenda

Project CEO Agenda
Half-day Professional Development

Creating Leadership Teams to Effectively Implement Academic Language Instruction through the Use of the ALL strategies

9:00–9:30 a.m.: Welcome / Present Program Goals
- Creating academic language awareness in teachers
- Increasing academic language proficiency for improved student outcomes
- Improving academic language instruction through ALL implementation
- Creating instructional leaders through a team-based approach

9:30–10:30 a.m.: Program Design: Teams, phases, and integration with existing initiatives

10:30 a.m.–12:00 p.m.: Discussion: requirements, benefits, and concerns

way of including their own learning to their existing practices. The benefit of this practice was evident when teachers shared how they incorporated the new learning to their practice at professional learning community (PLC) meetings.

In order to help implement with fidelity and to work through obstacles of implementation, it is key to work with the professional developers constantly. In Project CEO, the authors immersed themselves in the school three days per month to help teachers with planning, to observe, and to coach teachers. Specifically, the authors utilized their first visit in the month for planning meetings. On this day, teachers would meet with the authors to discuss their plans for implementation for the month and discuss lesson plans and how to incorporate ALL strategies. During the following two weeks (one visit per week), the authors would visit classrooms, observe, and meet individually with teachers to provide very specific implementation feedback.

The CEOs at each school had an essential role in developing the schedules for planning, observation, and feedback. During the school visits, the authors were also available to co-teach, co-plan, and model lessons as requested and needed.

Expectation 2. Teachers will engage in peer coaching. This expectation is the hardest to implement consistently; however, when it is implemented, the level of professionalism and implementation grows exponentially. There are often many barriers to coordinating peer observations such as testing preparation, classroom coverage, lack of time to meet prior to or after observing, and perceived lack of importance to this process. The CEO needs to take this expectation as a nonnegotiable and provide the organizational support to get teachers together for peer coaching.

The practice of peer coaching needs scaffolding for implementation. The authors found that the peer coaching process needs to be clearly outlined and understood. Next, teachers needed to practice peer coaching with support from the authors. Being present at the first peer coaching sessions helped teachers practice and apply the use of the coaching materials and the language of coaching. After this, peer coaches often continued the practice as long as the CEO required a reflection or written evidence of their coaching sessions.

Evidence of reflections and coaching are useful qualitative data of teacher development. CEOs need to read the evidence and provide feedback to the peer coaching teams. Peer coaching teams often look forward to this feedback and start using feedback more meaningfully to improve their practice. Common forms of evidence are summaries of pre-observation conference minutes, observation rubrics with comments, and post-observation reflections.

It is important to note that the frequency of monthly peer observations varies per CEO and school. Project CEO expected each team of two teachers to observe each other monthly; this turned out to be difficult to accomplish. A modification that worked in Project CEO was for the teams to take turns observing on a monthly basis. More concretely, one teacher in the pair observed one month; the next month this teacher was observed.

Expectation 3. Teachers and administrators will engage in monthly reflections. Reflecting on practice with peers provides many learning opportunities. Teachers who discuss their implementation and share the results of implementation, including successes and challenges, are on a path of continuous professional improvement.

The CEO and professional developers should find creative and meaningful activities to provide a framework for reflection. In Project CEO, the authors often used ALL strategies to help frame reflections. Teachers engaged in strategies found in chapter 3 to process their reflections. The authors found that practicing ALL strategies such as completing graphic organizers, four-squares, or sentence frames provided meaningful oppor-

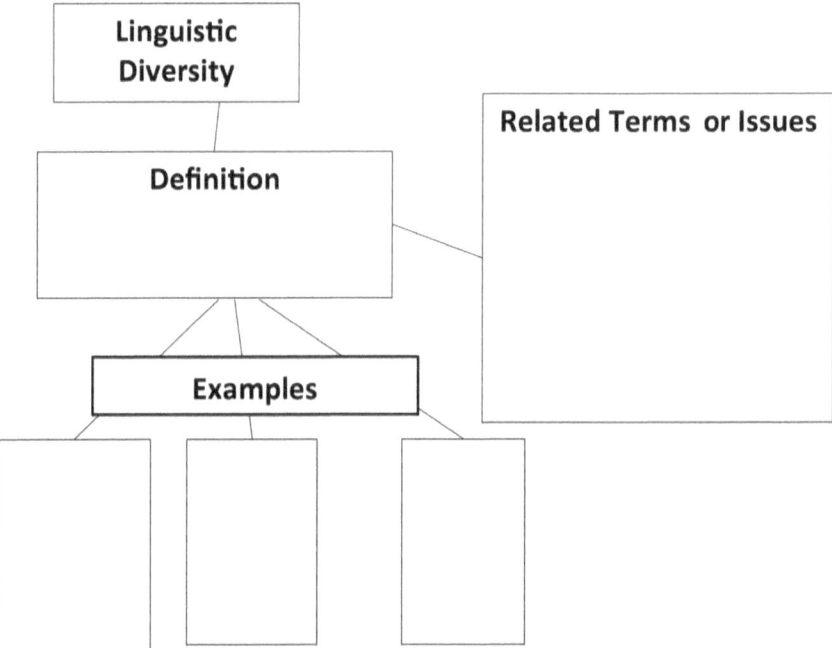

Figure 5.1. Sample Reflection Graphic Organizer

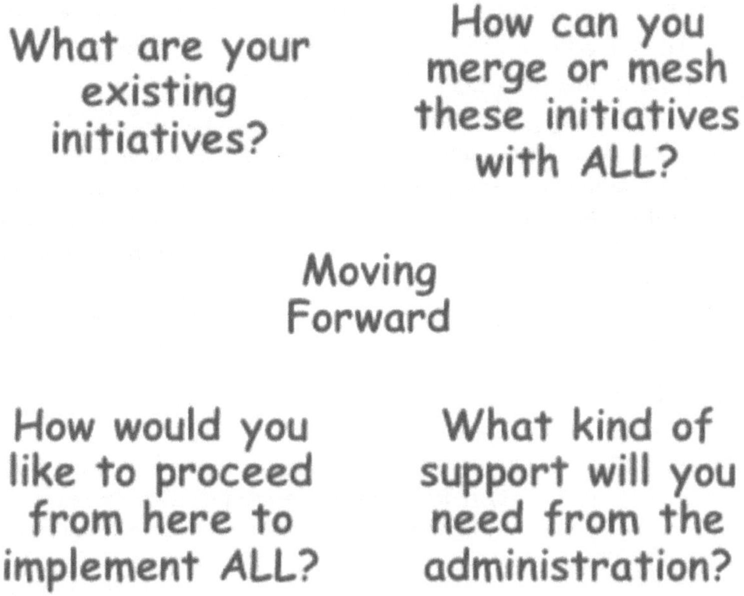

Moving Forward

- What are your existing initiatives?
- How can you merge or mesh these initiatives with ALL?
- How would you like to proceed from here to implement ALL?
- What kind of support will you need from the administration?

Figure 5.2. Sample Four-Square Reflection on Integration of ALL with Existing Initiatives

tunities for reflection as well as practice using ALL strategies. Figures 5.1 and 5.2 provide a sample graphic organizer and a sample four-square used to reflect on peer coaching and ALL integration with other initiatives.

Expectation 4. A team of teachers leads whole-group training each month. Once a month the entire team of participants meets to learn new content and reflect on their month's activities. In Project CEO, each pair of teachers was responsible for learning and teaching a component of the professional development once during the school year. This practice is essential because it promotes buy-in by the participants as teachers engage in a leadership role in their own professional learning.

In Project CEO, the university faculty modeled the first month of activities, the next month the team that presented included one with a principal, and the following months the teams took turns. To facilitate this practice, a sign-up sheet was completed at the first month's professional development after the trainers completed their modeling. Sometime during the month, prior to the training, the team of teachers that was to lead the whole-group training found time to plan their professional development and then met with the expert professional developers to discuss their plans and get feedback. Modifications to the month's professional development were incorporated based on feedback. Once the month's training was delivered to peers, the feedback to the team that led learning each month was used for the next month. Every opportunity for coaching is an opportunity for learning.

Expectation 5. Teachers and principals engage in ongoing professional learning by reading research and professional journals. Instructional leaders read and read often. Incorporating the practice of professional reading was essential to the project's success for two reasons: (1) teachers learn the habit of finding time to read professional journals and (2) teachers read from many credible sources about ALL and therefore see the relevance and importance of what they are learning. In Project CEO, the authors selected relevant articles that complemented the topic of the month and were written by national experts and published in highly readable journals such as *Educational Leadership*, *Phi Delta Kappan*, and *Journal of Staff Development*. In addition, ALL strategies were used to debrief the teachers' learning of the journal readings at the monthly professional development sessions. This provided an opportunity to practice and apply strategies that teachers could use in their classroom.

Organize Monthly Expectations

In Project CEO, the authors found it helpful for the CEO team to join a shared drive such as Dropbox or Google Drive and to include monthly folders with an outline for each month's activities. The shared drive also provided a place to store monthly journal articles and coaching activities. Additional resources, PowerPoints, and revisions to schedules were all stored in the shared drive that updates and syncs the information immediately to all participants. It is important to also take pictures to document ongoing progress. Pictures are a great source of evidence when sharing with others.

PHASE TWO: IMPLEMENTATION AND REFLECTION

The planning phase is essential to get buy-in, clarify the scope of work, and organize the different activities of the learning process. The implementation and reflection phase begins with professional development that provides an overview of ALL strategies and a preview of the types of teaching strategies participants will be learning and implementing. Project CEO scheduled an initial professional development during the weeks prior to starting the school year. The initial professional development length may vary. In this project the training took place over three days. The three days of professional development also served the purpose of getting to know the authors, establishing the expectations outlined in phase one, and understanding the concepts and skills of ALL strategies.

According to Guskey, this initial professional development is very important because the manner in which the project is introduced can excite participants or deter interest in continuing. Therefore, the initial professional development should be engaging, meaningful, and relevant to participants' work (2000, 94). Utilizing ALL strategies to deliver the professional development was an effective strategy for Project CEO. Participants were able to experience how the strategies helped them understand the content and scope of work and encouraged them to incorporate these strategies in their teaching.

Textbox 5.3 provides a sample agenda useful for delivering initial professional development. In this initial professional development, teachers tend to view the strategies as strategies they already implement. This is a common misconception for all that are learning new content. The strategies may be similar to those currently used; however, the difference is that the approach is on academic language acquisition strategies and most teachers do not learn language acquisition strategies as part of learning pedagogy.

The academic language acquisition strategies make sense and are similar to many used in teaching, yet there are specific linguistic rationales (see chapter 2) for strategies that need to become the focus of teachers as they plan and deliver their lessons. The point is, yes, teachers use strategies, but in ALL teachers use language strategies to teach content. For this reason, teachers need to realize that ALL will add to their existing repertoire of strategies the focus on academic language acquisition through various levels of proficiency.

Following the initial professional development, CEO teams from each school collaborated to apply their coaching and content knowledge throughout the school year. The yearlong professional development structures scaffold the content of the professional development by learning a major concept monthly and reviewing concepts learned cumulatively each month.

CEO teams met with the professional development experts three times each month and CEO principals facilitated peer observations and feedback opportunities on a weekly basis. The monthly structure (see table 5.6) of the professional development entailed planning and whole-group learning the first week of the month. During these whole-group meetings team

Textbox 5.3. Overview of Initial Professional Development

> **Project CEO Agenda**
>
> **August 7, 8, 9, 2012**
> Location: Tyrrell County Public Schools
> Using the ALL strategies to implement the Common Core Standards
>
> **August 7, 2012**
> 9:00–9:30 a.m.: Welcome / Present Three-Day Objectives
> 9:30–10:00 a.m.: Brief ALL overview and how ALL addresses the literacy strand of the common core
> 10:00 a.m.–11:30 a.m.: Integration of the Instruction Framework and the Writing Language Objectives
> - Addressing the components of the language objective
> - Addressing various language functions of the objective
> - Making Connections to the Common Core Literacy Focus
>
> 11:30 a.m.–12:30 p.m.: Lunch
> 12:30–3:30 p.m.: Facilitate working session to finalize integration and start developing course syllabi
>
> **August 8, 2012**
> 9–11:30 a.m.: Working session to finalize the integration of the Instructional Framework and the Strategies that address Academic Language development (for all students)
> 11:30 a.m.–12:30 p.m.: Lunch
> 12:30–3:30 p.m.: Facilitate working session to finalize integration and start developing course syllabi
>
> **August 9, 2012**
> 9:00–11:30 a.m.: Finalize integration of the Instruction Framework and the Strategies for teaching content vocabulary and Strategies for differentiating Academic Language Instruction
> 11:30 a.m.–12:30 p.m.: Lunch
> 12:30–3:30 p.m.: Facilitate working session to finalize integration and start developing course syllabi

members took turns presenting a component of ALL professional development, practiced coaching strategies using observations (both live and video recorded); engaged in study groups; discussed learning from peer feedback sessions; for half of the academic year featured a book discussion with the text *Academic Language for English Language Learners and Struggling Readers* (Freeman and Freeman 2009); and created supplementary materials such as manipulatives, crafts, and graphic organizers useful in making content instruction more comprehensible for students.

The next two weeks of each month, the CEO principals facilitated peer observations and feedback opportunities and CEO teachers implemented

Table 5.6. Sample Monthly Professional Development Activities

Times	Week 1 November 3 Planning Meetings	Week 2 November 10 Observations	Week 3 November 17 Observations or Planning	Week 4
Time	Week 1 Planning	Week 2 Observation Schedule	Week 3 Observation Schedule	Week 4 Authors' Planning Time
8:00–8:30	Travel from University			
8:30–9:00		Teacher 1— Middle School	Principals' meeting	
9:00–9:30		Teacher 2— Middle School		
9:30–10:00	Planning at Columbia Middle School (meet during common planning period)	Teacher A— Elem School	Teacher D— Elem School	
10:00–10:30			Teacher E— Elem School	
10:30–11:00		Teacher 3— Middle School		
11:00–11:30		Teacher 4— Middle School	Teacher 6— Middle School	
11:30–12:00		Teacher 5— Middle School	Teacher 7— Middle School	
12:00–12:30				
12:30–1:00	12:30–1:00pm Teacher A	Teacher B— Elem School		
1:00–1:30	1:00–1:30pm Teacher B 1:15–1:45pm Teacher C 1:45–2:15pm Teacher D 2:00–2:30pm Teacher E 2:30–3:00pm Teacher F	Teacher C— Elem School	Teacher F— Elem School	University Experts Planning time
1:30–2:00			Teacher G— Elem School	
2:00–2:30				
4:00–6:00	Whole Group Workshop			

ALL strategies in their teaching. One day a week within the two weeks, the university experts visited teachers, conducted observations, and provided feedback. It is important to note that the monthly schedule was developed collaboratively with the CEO principals and CEO teachers because the purpose is to develop trust and transparency, and to rely on the CEO team to find the times that work best for them. Each month the schedule was reviewed and modified based on the school activities and team responsibilities.

The CEO team exhibited the various stages of team building: forming, storming, norming, and performing (Tuckman and Jensen 1977). The team-building stage was embedded in the planning and initial professional development phase. Once the CEO team expectations became a reality, teams started the storming stage (which was developmentally a natural step). This storming stage was key in cementing the project protocols and changing teacher practice. This is the stage where the CEO principal conveys the message that implementation and peer feedback are nonnegotiable activities and thus the principal must facilitate these processes by modeling the process, being visible, providing feedback at every opportunity, and addressing the storming obstacles raised by teachers such as issues of time, resources, and personality conflicts.

The expert professional developers also must recognize the storming stage and use ALL strategies to clarify what coaching means. Teachers at this stage must feel that their teaching practices are not questioned or considered non-effective. Teachers at this stage need to get feedback on the implementation of ALL strategies that are new to all on the team.

In Project CEO, coaching was the process between two people in which exploration, critique, and reflection transformed practice. The interpersonal process is unique because each person has unique personalities and different professional experiences. Therefore the coaching process had general protocols and the CEO principals addressed personal storming issues since the principals had prior experience and strategies to work positively with their staff. A key message conveyed during this ongoing professional development is that trust was at the center of all interactions.

All feedback in Project CEO was meant for professional development and not meant for personal criticism. At the beginning, the teachers and professional developers had conversations about how feedback was taken, and changes were made to address the concerns. Each change cemented the trust aspect of the ongoing work. Finally, it is important that all members of CEO teams strive for positive change in instruction because the effect would be visible in student learning. The team's expectations were high and all for the betterment of student learning.

A monthly meeting with the CEO principals provided opportunities for planning, feedback, and a forum to share successes and concerns. Both principals and university faculty engaged in this meeting as an opportunity to use feedback to improve the ongoing professional development and reflection.

In addition to feedback opportunities outlined in this stage, at the end of the yearlong professional development, the CEO team reflected on the impact of implementation on classroom instruction of ELLs and SELs in their schools by conducting an internal formative evaluation of the effects of professional development using Guskey's five levels of professional development evaluations (see table 5.5). The CEO team utilized the data of the internal evaluation to shape the summer professional development and the activities for next year's implementation. This process is described in more detail in phase three.

PHASE THREE: CAPACITY BUILDING

Using the data collected in phases one and two, the CEO team developed their own professional development during summer months in order to train their entire school faculty. The authors provided coaching and mentoring during this phase. CEO team members delivered the training prior to beginning the next school year. The CEO principal then encouraged the professional learning community at the school to implement ALL strategies by following phases one and two as described in this chapter with the difference being that the experts in this stage were the CEO team that implemented the initial year and that also wrote professional development for the entire school staff.

AUTHORS' NOTE

The authors had every belief that their continued and intensive support would prove this work to be successful by the end of an academic year; however, the progress seen in the classrooms was overwhelmingly positive and rapid. Most teachers embraced ALL strategies and implemented them to a high level of fidelity. Those who appeared to struggle grew as well after they received one-on-one additional consultation with the authors. Due to the organizational structure of the middle school, students received ALL strategies in all of their content areas, thereby receiving intensive focus on academic language proficiency in all classes.

Even though the principals had busy schedules and did not have assistant principals, their dedication to Project CEO remained a high priority. This dedication is exactly what Project CEO is about, and the end result improved instruction in all classes impacted by the ALL strategies.

As a result of the budgetary changes, the authors were able to take four teachers who had never attended a national Teachers of English as a Second Language (TESOL) conference in New Orleans. These CEO teachers participated in workshops led by experts of the ALL strategies that they knew because they had implemented their strategies! At TESOL the CEO teams also met with the authors of an additional text used in training sessions in Project CEO. The opportunity to speak with the authors of this book about teaching and learning only intensified their professional desire to continue to implement ALL strategies. These four teachers evolved as the lead CEO teachers in their schools.

SUMMARY

The commitment to implementing ALL strategies should be reflected in the ongoing learning opportunities and the unrelenting push to embed ALL in professional practice. Professional development takes time and effort that teachers are willing to commit to when expectations of their time and promise of student achievement is clearly understood. The bottom line for integrating ALL into everyday practice is to learn from experts and then for teachers and principals to take ownership of their learning by practicing and applying.

WORKS CITED

Cummins, Jim. *Bilingualism and Special Education: Program and Pedagogical Issues*. Clevedon: Multilingual Matters, 1984.

Darling-Hammond, Linda. "What Matters the Most: A Competent Teacher for Every Child." *Phi Delta Kappan* 78 (1996): 193–200.

Freeman, Yvonne, and David Freeman. *Academic Language for English Language Learners and Struggling Readers: How to Help Students Succeed Across the Content Areas*. Portsmouth: Heinemann, 2009.

Guskey, Thomas. *Evaluating Professional Development*. Thousand Oaks: Corwin, 2000.

Hord, Shirley M., William L. Rutherford, and Leslie Huling-Austin. *Taking Charge of Change*. Austin: Southwest Educational Development Laboratory, 1987.

Joyce, Bruce, and Beverly Showers. *Student Achievement Through Staff Development: Fundamentals of School Renewal.* 2nd Edition. New York: Longman, 1998.

Learning Forward Professional Learning Association. *Standards for Professional Learning.* August 5, 2011. Accessed August 5, 2014. learningforward.org/standards-for-professional-learning.

Sparks, Dennis, and Stephanie Hirsh. *A New Vision for Staff Development.* Alexandria: Association for Supervision and Curriculum Development, 1997.

Tuckman, Bruce, and Mary Ann Jensen. "Stages of Small Group Development Revisited." *Group Organizational Studies* 2 (1977): 419–27.

❻

VISUALIZING CHANGE

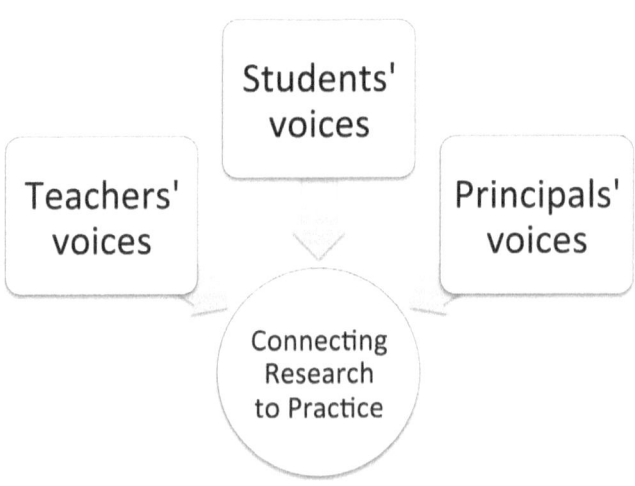

Chapter 6 Organizer

This final chapter shows how the research done through Project CEO has positively impacted the practice of teaching academic language literacy (ALL) at an elementary school, a middle school, and a high school. In order to exemplify the results, teachers', students', and principals' voices are shared. These reflections discuss the content, the context, and the process that have led to academic success for their students and teacher leadership for themselves.

PROJECT CEO SUMMARY

Project CEO was a professional development grant in partnership between the College of Education, the College of Arts and Sciences, at East Carolina University and Tyrrell County Schools, a small rural school system. The purpose of Project CEO was to change the perceived role of the principal from the "booking agent," the one who manages the building, the schedule, and the professional development to the "CEO—Chief Education Officer," the instructional leader who facilitates, leads, and participates in professional development for his or her school with the goal of improving student academic literacy across the content areas. Project CEO facilitated elementary, middle, and high school teams to be trained in ALL strategies, to meet weekly, and to have on-site visits from the authors of the book.

PARTICIPANTS AND PROFESSIONAL DEVELOPMENT: TYRRELL COUNTY

In Tyrrell County, the local economy attracts many immigrants for the fishing and agricultural industries. Many of the families that move to the area are English language learners. Tyrrell County is one of the most economically distressed counties in North Carolina. The level of poverty is reflected in the public schools in that 80 percent of their students receive free or reduced lunch. In addition, due to the high poverty levels, the level of formal education in the community is extremely low.

Tyrrell County public school system is one of the smallest in the state, with only one elementary, middle, and high school. Due to its small size and its rural location, the school system receives limited per-student resources. The school system is the largest employer in the county, housing the majority of college graduates for Tyrrell County. As a result, most children come from homes with low literacy rates and are entering schools with limited vocabulary and academic exposure.

Approximately 14 percent of their student population is Hispanic and the remainder of the population is equally divided between African Americans and Whites. There is an increasing trend in ELL growth with students from Hispanic and Vietnamese backgrounds. In 2012 pre-kindergarten ELL enrollment alone grew from 30 percent to 50 percent. This diverse student population creates a large number of regional nonstandard dialects in addition to the number of nonnative speakers. Teachers in the school system are forced to be both mainstream and ESL teachers; there is only one ESL teacher for three schools.

ELLs do not represent the only challenge to the teachers in Tyrrell County. Freeman and Freeman identify a second group of learners: Standard English Learners (SELs) (2009, 10). These are native English speakers whose dialects are nonstandard and whose home languages differ structurally from standard academic English. This represents a more common type of linguistic diversity, which is compounded by a lack of the appropriate background knowledge for school settings. The lack of background knowledge creates a deficiency of academic vocabulary, limiting full access to the curriculum (Marzano 2004).

At the time that Project CEO was implemented, over 65 percent of teachers had over ten years of teaching experience at the same location. Due to the isolation of this district from urban and developed areas, they had limited opportunities to participate in professional development without great personal expense. Therefore, it is implied that these teachers had little to no continuing education since their undergraduate teacher education over ten years before. Due to this phenomenon, they had not received additional training in "content-based strategies" for ELLs and SELs.

Project CEO relied heavily on ongoing and job-embedded professional development. Table 6.1 provides an average number of contact hours per participant.

Table 6.1. Average Numbers of Contact Hours per Participant

Participant	Contact Hours	Comments	Average Students per Teacher	Total Students
Principals	81	108 contact hours with elem & middle principals resulted in higher implementation		598
Elementary Teachers	62		17	
Middle School Teachers	68.75		67	
High School Teachers	27.5	Significantly less contact due to hurricane Irene resulted in less implementation	12	

PROFESSIONAL DEVELOPMENT FLEXIBILITY

During the first year of Project CEO, the school district that was initially planning to work with the authors changed at the last minute. This school district had massive principal reassignments in midsummer 2010. Among these changes were the two principals who had worked to develop this project. Attempts were made to immediately contact and work with the newly assigned principals; however, the project objectives were no longer a priority at these schools. The superintendent clearly supported her teachers and principals in their decision not to follow through with Project CEO. This decision was made two weeks before the initial professional development workshop, leaving the authors with funding, materials already developed and purchased, and no schools.

The authors contacted the superintendent of Tyrrell County schools, as they were a high-need school district. After two meetings and numerous phone calls and e-mails, the authors established a new team with whom to collaborate. The two principals from the elementary and middle school exhibited enthusiasm, willingness, and flexibility to ensure the success of Project CEO and the academic growth of their students. The superintendent was an exceptional supporter throughout the project.

During the second year of Project CEO, when the high school joined the project, Hurricane Irene forced closure of the schools on August 29, which was the initial visit after the summer training. Schools remained closed for a week and a half. Hurricane Irene devastated the middle and high school buildings along with many of the materials that were purchased by Project CEO. Among the items lost in the two feet of floodwaters were the books purchased for professional development. Any materials that survived the flood were in storage units that were not accessible and the inventory of damaged school supplies included many of the project items.

Even though the authors had seen this information in the news and spoken to teachers and administrators over the phone, one could not fully imagine how deeply this had affected instruction. Normalcy did not return to Tyrrell County for at least three months. The middle school returned to its original building a week before Thanksgiving, after being relocated to a conference center in the area. Upon their return, teachers attempted to teach without materials or classroom doors.

The high school's campus lost approximately a third of its usable space and had teachers doubled up in the media center, cafeteria, gym, and classrooms. Due to the adverse teaching conditions and emotional and personal impact on teachers and students, Project CEO was at the bottom of their priority list.

The authors continued to visit teachers and provide encouragement, informal feedback, and guidance in trying to get started with ALL implementation.

The elementary and middle school teachers who had participated the previous year in Project CEO were able to continue their work without much impact; however, the high school teachers had a harder time getting started. The principals were very preoccupied with building management and supported the authors' efforts as best they could under the circumstances. After the winter break, readings, discussions, observations, and meetings were better able to focus on the project goals.

Unexpected Favorable Outcomes

The authors had every belief that continued and intensive support would prove this professional development to be successful by the end of the each academic year; however, with delays in starting the implementation phase the odds were not favorable. These obstacles were quickly overcome once implementation began. The progress seen in classrooms was overwhelmingly positive and rapid in spite of the rocky and late start. Most teachers embraced the ALL strategies and implemented with a high level of fidelity. Those who appeared to struggle grew as well after they received one-on-one additional feedback and coaching.

ACCOMPLISHMENTS AND OUTCOMES

Outcome 1. Participants increased their knowledge and pedagogical skills in teaching academic language to ELLs and SELs. All participants (100 percent) completed a Sheltered Instruction Observation Protocol (SIOP®) self-assessment, the ALL model used in this project (see chapter 2), prior to the initial professional development and at the end of the academic year. Initially, all indicated limited to no knowledge of the SIOP® model. The model was implemented by learning about one of the eight components each month. In comparing the pre- and post-assessments, 100 percent of the participants showed increased knowledge of the SIOP®.

All teachers provided copies of a lesson plan prior to learning about ALL. Upon reviewing the lesson plans, it was evident that teachers were not previously implementing ALL strategies. During Project CEO, each month teachers' plans indicated strategies that aligned with the component of the month. Upon review of their final lesson plans, it was evident that 95 percent of the participants developed comprehensive ALL-infused lesson plans.

Outcome 2: Project CEO provided sustained high-quality professional development when coaching and providing follow-up for ALL activities to improve ELL and SEL content-area achievement. CEO team members practiced coaching skills consistently. Elementary school participants implemented ALL strategies when teaching their daily mathematics lesson. Middle school and high school participants implemented the ALL strategies in all of their classes. The authors visited all classrooms and completed observation-rating forms to determine the level of implementation of ALL strategies. The feedback from the observations was shared with each participant the same day of the observation. From mid-fall semester after the initial training to final observations there was a marked difference in classroom practices targeting academic language development.

Participants reflected on lesson planning and delivery, their peer observations, and assigned monthly professional journal articles in writing. The authors reviewed the journals on a monthly basis. On final review of the portfolios, it was evident that all teachers had adopted academic language literacy strategies and now focused on planning and teaching content-based instructional practices.

Outcome 3: Project CEO enhanced CEO leadership skills as instructional leaders and developed teacher leaders. On a monthly basis, CEO members and their partners presented an ALL topic of the month to the whole group at an after-school workshop. All participants consistently provided feedback via instructional conversations.

The principals and the authors presented at the National Council of Professors of Educational Administration in August 2011. The audience for this conference included professors in school administration as well as superintendents and principals nationwide.

The authors were able to take four teachers who had never attended a national conference to the Teachers of English as a Second Language (TESOL) conference in New Orleans. These teachers were able to participate in workshops led by the developers of the SIOP® and the authors of an additional text used in training sessions. These four teachers have evolved as the lead ALL teachers in their schools.

Outcome 4: CEO team members took a leadership role in delivering high quality ALL professional development school-wide after their own yearlong implementation was completed using materials developed in Project CEO. Six participants (four teachers, two principals) developed their own ALL professional development workshop with the assistance of the authors during the summer of 2011. In August 2011 this was presented school-wide.

The next sections share voices from the participants of Project CEO. ALL strategies were implemented school-wide the next year following Project CEOs implementation plan.

TEACHERS' VOICES

Understanding the overall goal of professional development is essential. During phase one, preparation and planning, a recommended practice is to engage in an overview professional development to understand the content of the professional development. At the conclusion of the initial SIOP® professional development during summer 2010, Project CEO participants provided feedback of their understanding and concerns to the authors by completing four simple sentence starters: (1) "I came expecting . . . "; (2) "I got . . . "; (3) "Now I hope . . . "; and (4) "Now I need to . . ." These responses were coded as themes emerged. Participants' comments indicated a strong desire to implement SIOP® in the classes for the benefit of all learners, but also acknowledge perceived challenges for implementation.

Teachers' experiences during coaching sessions provided valuable insight on implementation and concerns. Analysis of reflective feedback from the monthly coaching sessions provided valuable insight into the perceptions of the participants. Data analyzed included a written survey and field notes. The evolution of the quality of the feedback was compelling. Exemplar

Table 6.2. Teachers' Voices about Initial Professional Development

Themes from Initial SIOP® Training Feedback		
Sentence Starters	Theme (# of responses)	Exemplar Quote(s)
I came expecting . . .	Learn about the SIOP® model (8)	I came expecting to learn about the SIOP®. Learn specific SIOP® activities and Strategies.
	Learn about teaching ELLs or struggling learners (4)	To learn about ELLs and how they struggle in the classroom. Strategies to help struggling learners.
	Another teaching requirement (3)	I came expected to be overwhelmed with paperwork. More work that I would have to do.
	No idea what to expect (3)	Clueless. Boring lecture. Didn't really know what to expect.

Themes from Initial SIOP® Training Feedback		
Sentence Starters	Theme (# of responses)	Exemplar Quote(s)
I got . . .	Understanding of the SIOP® model and teaching strategies within the model (13)	A better understanding about the purpose of the SIOP® and how this will improve my teaching. Increasing understanding of morphology.
	Understanding about language acquisition (5)	How it (the SIOP®) is beneficial to SELs as well as ELLs. Many strategies and many ways to implement them with ELL students.
	Workshop presentation comments (2)	A great day, fast-paced, active participation. A written list of meeting dates and assignment expectations.
Now I hope . . .	Positive plans to implement (10)	I hope to implement these strategies in the classroom. Become a better teacher and reach all students more effectively.
	Become a teacher leader (2)	I hope I become an effective SIOP® teacher and leader. To learn how to help my teachers help students learn.
	Organizational and implementation challenges (4)	I hope I don't get stressed out. Allow sufficient time to complete everything. I hope teachers accept this challenge and see the benefits.
Now I need to . . .	Spend time planning for implementation (12)	Get organized. Prepare myself using books provided. Apply strategies in classroom. Talk more with my partners about the SIOP®.
	Other comments (2)	Get some rest. Clone myself.

quotes in table 6.3 denote the thematic responses across the monthly meetings, illustrating the change in concerns and activities of the Project CEO teachers over time.

The feedback evolved from a focus on preparation for the SIOP® implementation to a focus on action. Across the monthly meetings the coaching conversations shifted from informational and "how-to" themes to implementation and instructional strategy themes. These participant reactions demonstrate the relevance of the Project CEO activities to their classroom practice and participants' engagement in the professional development activities.

Table 6.3. Teachers' Voices about Peer Coaching

Themes from Coaching Sessions Feedback and Field Notes					
		Theme Frequency			
Question 1	Theme	Oct	Nov	Dec	Feb
During this month's collaborative planning meeting, how did you help your partner prepare for this month's SIOP® component?	Discussed ideas and gave feedback	8	10	14	12
	Focused on comprehensible input	6	8	12	12
	Did not meet	5	3	1	0
	Adapted instruction for those with different backgrounds	7	12	14	14
	Strategized to promote interaction/incorporate SIOP® model	4	10	14	13
Question 2		Oct	Nov	Dec	Feb
How did you provide comprehensible feedback? Please give examples and discuss any problems that may have arisen.	Communicated via e-mail	6	8	10	13
	Discussed and threw ideas back and forth	7	12	10	22
	Used hands-on activities to engage students	8	10	13	14
	Had difficulty communicating	7	4	1	1
	Vented to each other	8	12	8	4
Question 3		Oct	Nov	Dec	Feb
Based on your coaching session and meetings, what do you take away that will help you better coach this component of the SIOP®?	Understood SIOP®/comprehensible input component better	12	12	12	14
	Worked together	11	12	12	13
	Implemented hands-on activities for classroom engagement	7	12	14	14
	Acknowledged that planning is necessary	6	11	12	14
	Became more aware of speech in the classroom (too fast, loud, etc.)	8	12	12	14
	Became more aware of the number of strategies to use and also became more open to ideas	10	12	13	14
	Knew what to look for when completing an observation	1	4	7	14

CEO teachers commented about the school leadership and their efforts to help support implementation. Themes for the school leadership and implementation are shown in table 6.4.

Table 6.4. Teachers' Voices about Project CEO's Impact on Teaching and Learning

Themes from Coaching Session Feedback		
Questions	Theme (# of reponses)	Exemplar Quote(s)
How has participation changed classroom practices?	Project CEO has made my teaching more "Student-Centered" (6)	Moving away from teacher-centered classroom to a student-centered classroom. Letting the students take control has been the biggest difference in my classroom.
	New ideas to implement in the classroom/instructional techniques (3)	I am constantly seeking new ways to get my students engaged in learning; even on my lunch break I am thinking and searching the Internet.
	More reflective about teaching practice (2)	Project CEO has changed my classroom practice because I am more reflective about my teaching practice.
	Students are really learning/ learning academic language (2)	My students participate in groups more frequently. They are learning to speak the academic language so building background in another subject or grade will come easier.
Has Project CEO changed the role of your principal with regards to instructional leadership? Please Explain.	No change in our principal's leadership (5)	I have not noticed any change in the leadership. I don't know that I have seen much difference because she has always been supportive.
	Principal has become more of a coach/instructional leadership (2)	My principal has become more of a coach in my school's mission to provide the best academic opportunities for students.
	Focuses on classroom and teaching being student centered (5)	The principal is still involved but is having more conversations geared toward strategies and student-centered learning.
	Allows time to collaborate to work through strategies (1)	Allows time to collaborate (use of professional development) to work through strategies

An open-ended questionnaire completed by CEO teachers about the role of their school principal in Project CEO provided evidence for organizational support and change. The themes that emerged from this questionnaire fell into three main categories.

- First, Project CEO principals served as active participants in the ALL implementation. They attend training sessions, facilitated ALL observations, and even led lessons.
- Second, Project CEOs fostered an environment for success. Principals provided time and space for the ALL implementation to take root and become successful through ALL planning days, facilitated observations, and resources support. They also discussed Project CEO at formal and informal meetings at the school, increasing the visibility of the project and highlighting the leadership role Project CEO teachers were taking.
- Third, Project CEO principals enhanced their leadership skills by showing trust in the skills and expertise of their teachers. One teacher's comment summarized these themes: "There was a change in my principal. I know she believed in her teachers. She had faith in us that we would do what needed to be done. She gave us support, encouragement, and time to collaborate with other colleagues."

Table 6.5. Teachers' Voices about the Principal Becoming a CEO

Themes from Organizational Support and Change Feedback		
Question	Theme (# of responses)	Exemplar Quote(s)
Is the principal an active and enthusiastic learner? If so, how have you seen this in this yearlong SIOP® professional development?	Principal is actively engaged in SIOP® trainings and classrooms (3) Read all SIOP® books and participated in discussions (2) Provided substitutions for days teachers needed to catch up on SIOP® work (2)	She has been present at every afternoon meeting and has even taught SIOP® lessons to students as well. She provided us with the materials we needed to make the program work and assisted in developing and teaching lessons that supported the SIOP® model.
Does the principal work with you to improve your implementation of SIOP® in the classroom? Explain.	Principal provided strategies and help for teachers/feedback (3) Provided time to work on SIOP® implementation (2)	Yes, she has come in and observed our classes and has recommended different strategies that might work better. She has ordered materials that we have requested for our students. She has given us a day to plan with our co-teachers.

Themes from Organizational Support and Change Feedback		
Question	Theme (# of responses)	Exemplar Quote(s)
Does the principal encourage peer coaching to help you learn the SIOP®? If so, provide examples.	Encouraged teacher collaboration (2) Allowed teacher to observe each other in the classroom (3) Permitted teachers to have planning days (2)	She also encourages other teachers to observe in SIOP® classrooms so we can begin coaching others.
Are the results of the SIOP® shared with all staff members of the school? If so, how?	Sharing SIOP® with colleagues in formal and informal settings (3) Constantly discuss SIOP® with other teachers (3)	We have discussed SIOP® at faculty meetings, invited other staff members in our classroom to see our work, and talk about it in our team meetings.
Was there a change in your principal during the yearlong professional development? If so, expound.	Principal demonstrated more faith in teacher's work (2) No change in principal—always been encouraging and supportive (4) Principal has been excited to see test results and success rates (1)	There was a change in my principal. I know she believed in her teachers. She had faith in us that we would do what needed to be done. She gave us support, encouragement, and time to collaborate with other colleagues. I wouldn't say there was a change. She has always been willing to come in our classrooms to observe and assist in any way we needed her. She is also available to help whenever we need her.
How could the principal continue to help with the SIOP® going school-wide?	Continues to support the program (4) Continued encouragement and sharing (2) Offer training to any new staff and also work with the high school teacher (1)	She should continue to be an active member in the process. If we see her so involved in the process it makes the teachers more involved as well.

Project CEO teachers completed a summative survey to assess their opinions of student learning outcomes in May 2011. Table 6.6 reports feedback items addressing cognitive and affective elements of student learning and student engagement and the overall impact of Project CEO and the SIOP® implementation. Cognitive question feedback focused on students and highlighted improved student comprehension and achievement.

Affective question feedback overlapped with cognitive question feedback in the area of student engagement in learning, but went a step further by addressing student motivation for learning. For example, an elementary teacher remarked, "My students have taken an attitude that their learning is important. They have also taken on the responsibility to be self-learners."

Table 6.6. Teachers' Voices about Student Learning Outcomes

Themes from Summative Teacher Feedback		
Feedback	Theme (# of responses)	Exemplar Quote(s)
Cognitive	Improved instruction (1)	SIOP® has helped me provide a stronger background for my students.
	Improved student test scores (2)	When reviewing my grade book and student samples I can see that the scores are higher than before I used SIOP®. My students have begun to use the academic language in my classroom in conversations with each other.
	Improved comprehension (3)	They use the academic language that goes along with the content and it sticks with them. They find these words sometimes in their leisure reading and begin to discuss with me when and why they learned that content.
Cognitive B	No achievement differences between ELLs and English speaking students (4)	I have not seen a significant difference between my LEP students and English-speaking students, as out of four LEP students in my classroom, two are my highest students and the other two are my lowest students.
	Both groups have shown improvement (2)	I do feel that my LEP students are performing higher after using the SIOP® and also my English-speaking students. Both groups of students showed improvements in their class work, homework, test, and overall participation in class.
Affective A	Student engagement (4)	They love working with groups on activities that are still getting the content to them. They would rather do an activity with a group of students they normally do not communicate with instead of me standing in front of the room lecturing them.
	Student motivation (2)	The students are more motivated and enjoy learning, especially if they are doing group work or working with a partner. They are excited to learn from each other. Oh, yes! My students have taken an attitude that their learning is important. They have also taken on the responsibility to be self-learners.

\	Themes from Summative Teacher Feedback	
Feedback	Theme (# of responses)	Exemplar Quote(s)
Affective B	Student work group dynamics (6)	Before SIOP®, I would have one or two students in the group that would do all the work and the others would just sit back and talk—not anymore!! Now they all want to know!
Unintended Outcomes	None (1)	No, cannot think of any.
	Students' use and awareness of academic language (2)	The students learned how important it is to use academic language and they began correcting each other.
	Improved Socialization (2)	Students who tend to be withdrawn and never speak out in class excel in small groups because it is a safe environment with their peers.
	Students more engaged in learning (1)	SIOP® has helped my students develop into new learners. They are engaged in their learning and taking a greater responsibility for their actions.
Measurable Outcomes	Difficult to measure impact, suggestions offered (5)	By looking at involvement in classroom and data you can see development of students. Documenting conversations as students corrected each other. Documented through reflections and conversations with parents and principal.
Positive/ Negative Outcomes	Positive Outcomes (5)	These are positive outcomes, because in the future they will be well prepared to use the academic language expected in the upper grades.
	Students will be more prepared to use the academic language in the future (2)	I would consider these positive outcomes! The students are learning not only academic language but to listen to each other. That in itself is a great improvement for middle school students!

STUDENTS' VOICES

The first year of implementation of Project CEO did not lead to overall increases in student achievement scores in reading and mathematics as measured on the end-of-grade tests. However, positive gains were made in test scores for ELLs and African American students at both Project CEO schools. These initial positive results may demonstrate the effectiveness of Project CEO and the implementation of the ALL strategies in these schools. When viewed in conjunction with the positive teacher perceptions of student achievement, these initial, small, increases in students' achievement scores among ELL and Black students are successes.

The notable gain in achievement occurred among students with disabilities. These students normally take several attempts to pass their standardized test (Extend 2) but for students in Project CEO schools, their pass rate was 100 percent on the first testing attempt. In addition, the average learning growth for students with disabilities surpassed the predicted scores by an average of fourteen points. Some students were not predicted to show growth; to everyone's surprise they all showed learning growth.

The second year of implementation of Project CEO resulted in an increase in student pass rate of Algebra 1, and also had only expected learning growth. Biology and English 1 pass rates decreased, but both of these had high learning growth. Because of the rural location of the high school, the student cohorts are small, and the students enter schools with low background knowledge and academically behind. So the pass rate dropped, yet growth increased, meaning the teachers did a good job moving the kids forward in their learning of academic language.

Similarly at the middle school, Math pass rates decreased; however, learning growth rates increased. Qualitative data collected from student focus groups indicated that students are more aware of the use of academic language and see a benefit in the use of content and language objectives in knowing what they are supposed to learn on a daily basis. The focus group discussion with students also indicated that students noticed a difference between teachers who were using ALL strategies and those who were not. Students indicated that they "looked forward" to learning in the classrooms that were implementing the ALL more than in other classrooms. Teacher interviews also revealed their perception that students engaged more meaningfully when they used ALL strategies within their lessons.

The daily routines implemented as part of the SIOP® model provided comforting structure for students. In Project CEO, teachers wrote both language and content objectives in student-friendly language. Content objectives began with the sentence starter, "Today I will learn . . ." and language objectives began with the sentence starter, "My job today is . . ." When students were asked to respond to this question, "I like when we read . . ." "Today we will learn . . ." and "My job today is . . . ," 61 percent of students responded positively.

Subsequent open-ended questions provided a rich picture of teacher practice in the Project CEO classrooms. As evidenced by the exemplar quotes, the language used by students in their responses reflected the use of academic language by Project CEO teachers in their classrooms. While the feedback questionnaire did not ask students to reflect upon their academic achievement directly, their responses do suggest that students are internalizing learning strategies that will benefit them in their future education.

Table 6.7. Students' Voices about Project CEO

Themes from Summative Student Feedback			
SIOP® Element	Feedback Question	Themes (# of Responses)	Exemplar Quote(s)
Preparation	How do the daily content and language objectives help me?	Preparation for learning (55) Do not help (19) Helps with grammar (17) Supports learning (24)	They tell what we are doing so I know how to be prepared.
Building Background	How does my teacher help me link new learning to my experiences in past learning?	Does not link (2) Uses previous year's examples (58) Reviews content (9) Uses variety of instructional activities (8) Uses new material (17)	We do a lot of comparing and contrasting. If we are reading a book, we might compare that character to a different character in a different book.
Comprehensible Inputs	How does my teacher emphasize key vocabulary?	Uses foldables and graphic organizers (26) Provides clear explanations (5) Repetition (13) Writing definitions (42)	She gives us many activities to do our vocabulary. She gives us a partner and we each act out a word and we write down the word and definition and then draw pictures.
Strategies	What does the teacher do to help me understand the concept?	Groupwork/partners (14) Additional discussion, explanation, repetition (41) Uses technology or games (30)	Teachers let us partner up and explain it more than one time.
Interactions	How often does your teacher provide opportunities to interact and discuss content with my peers?	Always (44) Sometimes (85) Never (0)	

(continued)

Table 6.7. (Continued)

Themes from Summative Student Feedback			
SIOP® Element	Feedback Question	Themes (# of Responses)	Exemplar Quote(s)
Practice/ Application	What helpful learning strategies do we use in class?	Groupwork/partners (39) Review/Review Games (14) Graphic organizers and Hands-on activities (36)	Four-squares, partner work, group work, clickers, technology, charts, and diagrams.

PRINCIPALS' VOICES

Principals were asked to identify, in their opinion, specific aspects that they provided for organizational support that contributed to the success of this SIOP® yearlong professional development. The high school principal indicated that the selection of the CEO teachers is essential. She stated that she "selected enthusiastic teachers and strong instructional leaders to pilot the SIOP® program at CHS." The middle school principal involved all teachers because the school is small and therefore the implementation was school-wide. The elementary principal selected one teacher per grade level.

Honest and open communication was key in the success of Project CEO. The authors also met with principals weekly, both formally and informally, and openly communicated their concerns and praises. Equally, principals picked up the phone and dialed the authors at any time to discuss progress, as did the authors.

In addition to selecting teachers, principals maintained high visibility throughout the project. The high school principal discussed her visibility, "I attended all sessions personally, and completed all readings/assignments: modeled appropriate behavior to participants." The middle school and elementary teachers shared similar comments. Another important strategy the principals shared was that they conducted classroom walk-throughs often and stopped to discuss implementation. The middle school principal shared that she often "looked for SIOP® strategies during classroom walk-throughs." The elementary principal shared that she sometimes sat in classrooms and "followed the teachers' lesson plans that were sitting at their desk. It was helpful to see the same language that had been discussed in professional development."

All three principals always shared that they would find the time to discuss their walk-through observation feedback the same day and that during formal observations they would find the time to ask questions and coach on ALL.

Principals were asked to think back to the implementation of SIOP® during the school year, and share what steps should be taken to ensure that they provide support more thoroughly for the upcoming school-wide implementation of SIOP®. The high school principal shared that she planned to "continue to emphasize how SIOP® and Common Instructional Framework are fully aligned and allow teachers to work with new pacing guides to integrate Common Core/Essential Standards with SIOP® prior to the start of the year." The middle and elementary school principals shared that teachers were going to continue their monthly learning community meetings and follow the professional development process used during Project CEO.

When principals were asked their opinion on student learning outcomes, the high school principal reviewed classroom assessment and shared that she noticed that "teachers are more aware of using academic language and teachers are using sentence starters, getting better written academic student responses." The high school principal also noted that teachers were "using more grouping activities in daily lessons, and students were doing well with these strategies." Both middle and elementary principals noticed academic language used frequently on the student work samples posted around the rooms and in the hallways. All three principals noticed students were excited about learning and walked into classrooms looking for content and language objectives.

SUMMARY

Professional development is a process that involves working with professional developers, teachers, administrators, and students. An effective professional development is one that offers meaningful opportunities to grow and develop as a professional; this includes ongoing implementation support in daily lessons. CEOs cannot provide this support alone. CEOs need to work with partners to develop teachers. This book proposes forming partnerships with universities to promote student success. This book also explains that focusing on academic language literacy, teachers can improve student learning. This focus occurs when teachers study and analyze the language of their content (vocabulary, process, and morphology) and incorporate instructional strategies that focus on academic language acquisition. The voices shared in this chapter portray a picture of teachers', students', and administrators' perceptions of effective professional development. More importantly, the experiences embedded in Project CEO's professional development resulted in developing instructional leadership skills for principals and teachers.

AUTHORS' NOTE

We feel that Project CEO learning and the constant reflecting was key in making teachers feel confident about their professionalism, which adds to their teacher leadership. Traveling with teachers and principals to a conference was also important because teachers got to see the authors as professors, as normal people, and as parents. Project CEO helped cement a lifelong friendship with teachers and administrators in Tyrrell County. We are no longer just professors from ECU; we are part of their teaching support structure! One of the authors passed away in April 2013 and even though she is missed dearly her message is present in Tyrrell County.

WORKS CITED

Freeman, Yvonne, and David Freeman. *Academic Language for English Language Learners and Struggling Readers: How to Help Students Succeed Across the Content Areas.* Portsmouth: Heinemann, 2009.

Marzano, Robert. *Building Background Knowledge for Academic Achievement: Research on What Works in Schools.* Alexandria: Association of Supervision and Curriculum Development, 2004.

www.ingramcontent.com/pod-product-compliance
Lightning Source LLC
Chambersburg PA
CBHW030117010526
44116CB00005B/291